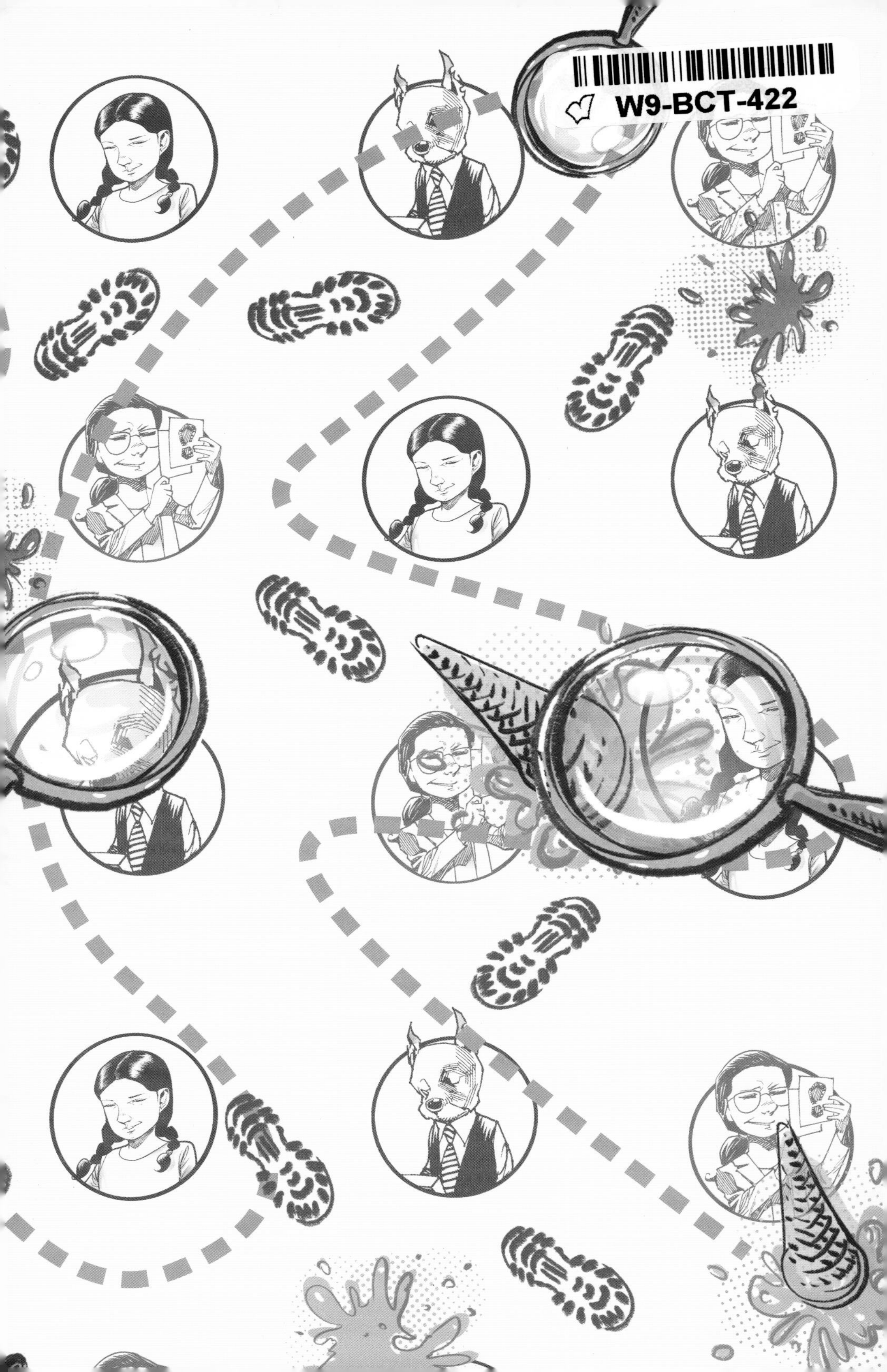

THE REZ++ DETECTIVES

Clifton Park - Halfmoon Public Library
475 Moe Road
Clifton Park, NY 12065

Published by Literati Press Comics & Novels
3010 Paseo, Oklahoma City, OK 73103
Find us online at literatipressok.com & @literatipress

Hardcover ISBN: 978-1-943988-33-4

Penciled, Inked, and Colored by M.K. Perker
Cover art by Cynthia Canada
Edited by Charles J. Martin, Chloe Harrison, and Steve Gooch
Book design by Jonathan Koelsch & Charles J. Martin

First Edition, 2021
Printed in the United States of America

This one, as with most things in my life, is for Nuseka Jacob—a strong person who is still the best of all of us. This book is also dedicated to all those crazy rez kids all over the world. Whether you're young or young at heart, simply by existing you have made the universe a better place.

–Tvli Jacob

REZ DOG

DETECTIVE AGENCY

STEVEN PAUL JUDD, TVLI JACOB & M.K. PERKER

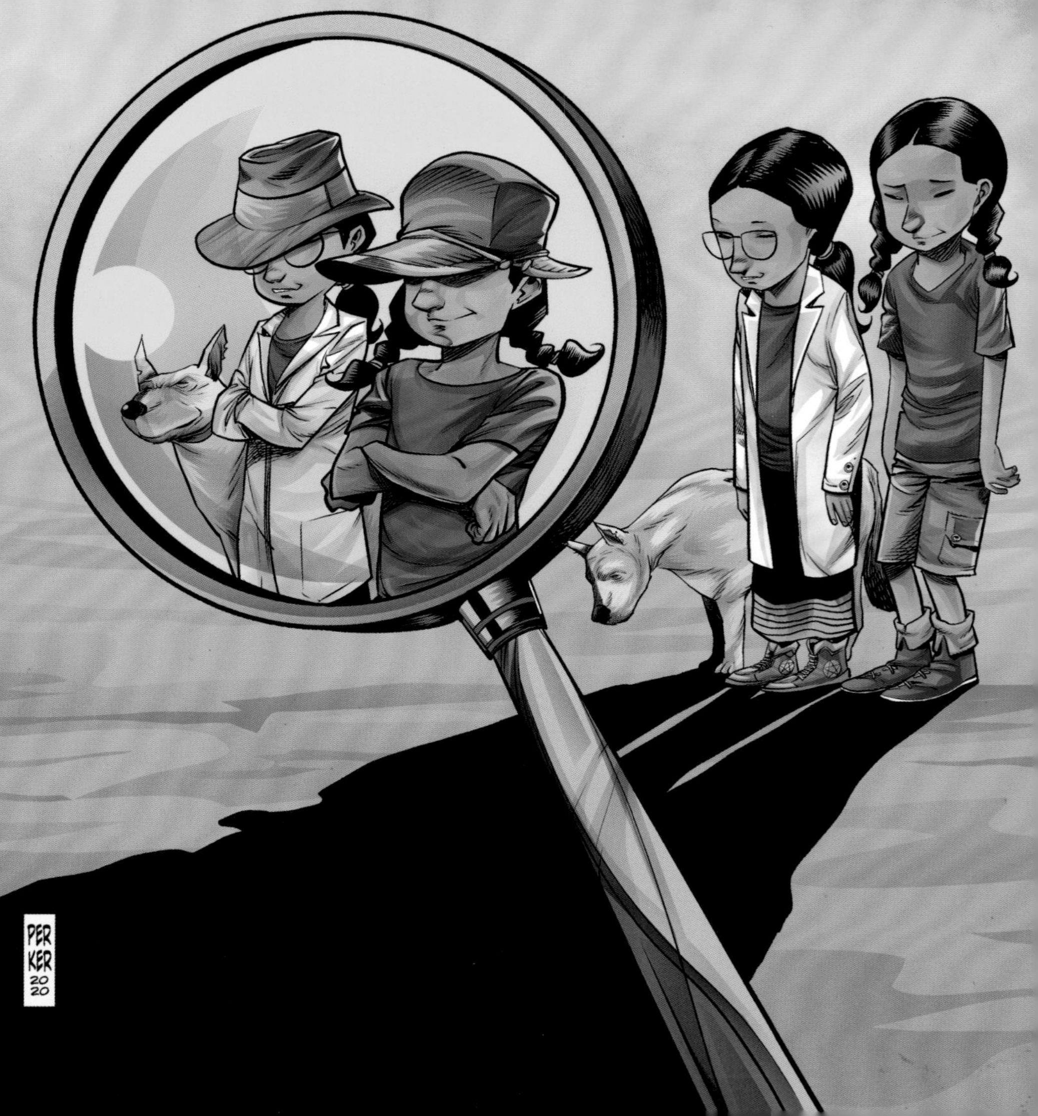
PER
KER
2020

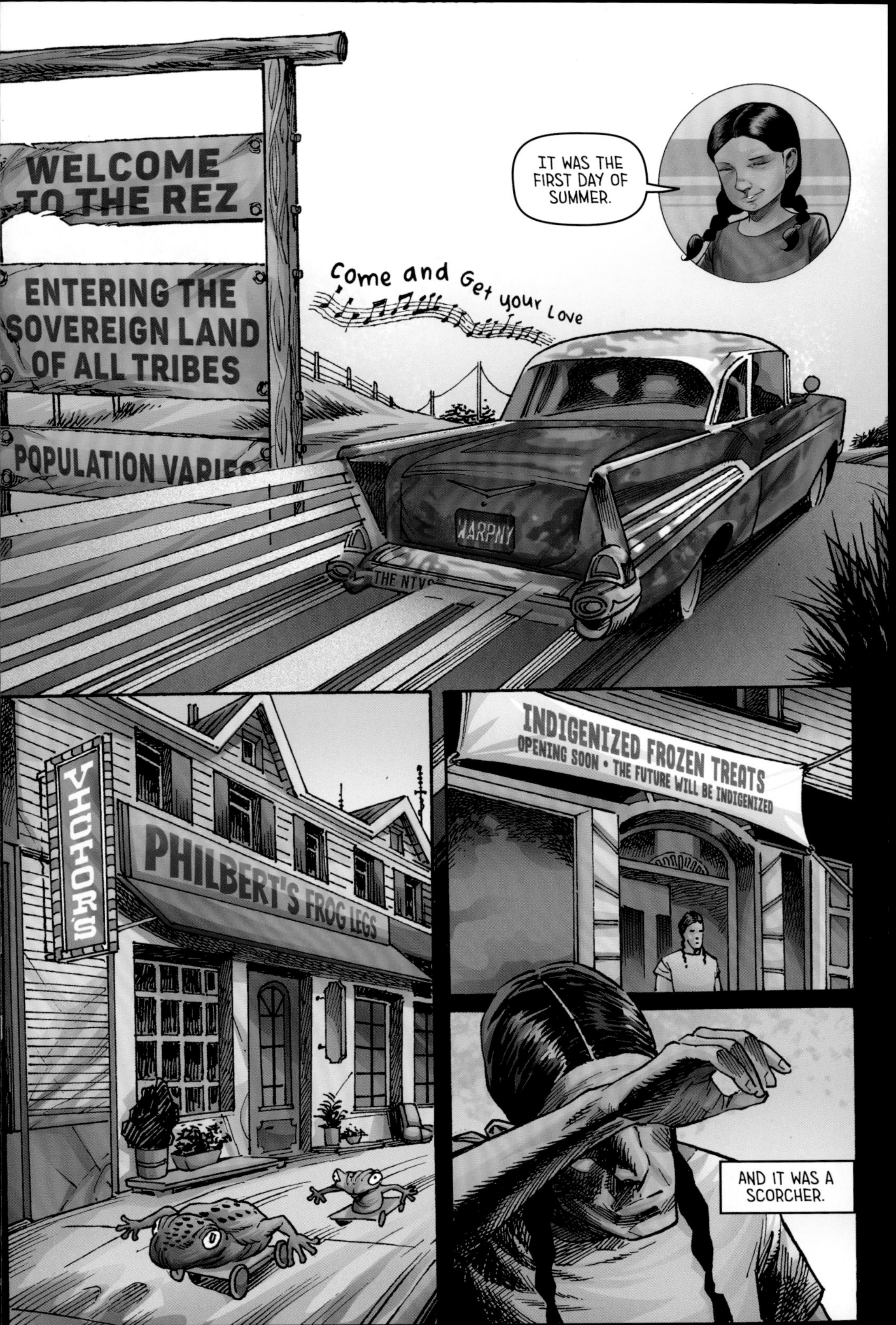
IT WAS THE FIRST DAY OF SUMMER.
WELCOME TO THE REZ
ENTERING THE SOVEREIGN LAND OF ALL TRIBES
POPULATION VARIES
Come and Get your Love
WARPNY
THE NTVS
VICTOR'S
PHILBERT'S FROG LEGS
INDIGENIZED FROZEN TREATS
OPENING SOON • THE FUTURE WILL BE INDIGENIZED
AND IT WAS A SCORCHER.

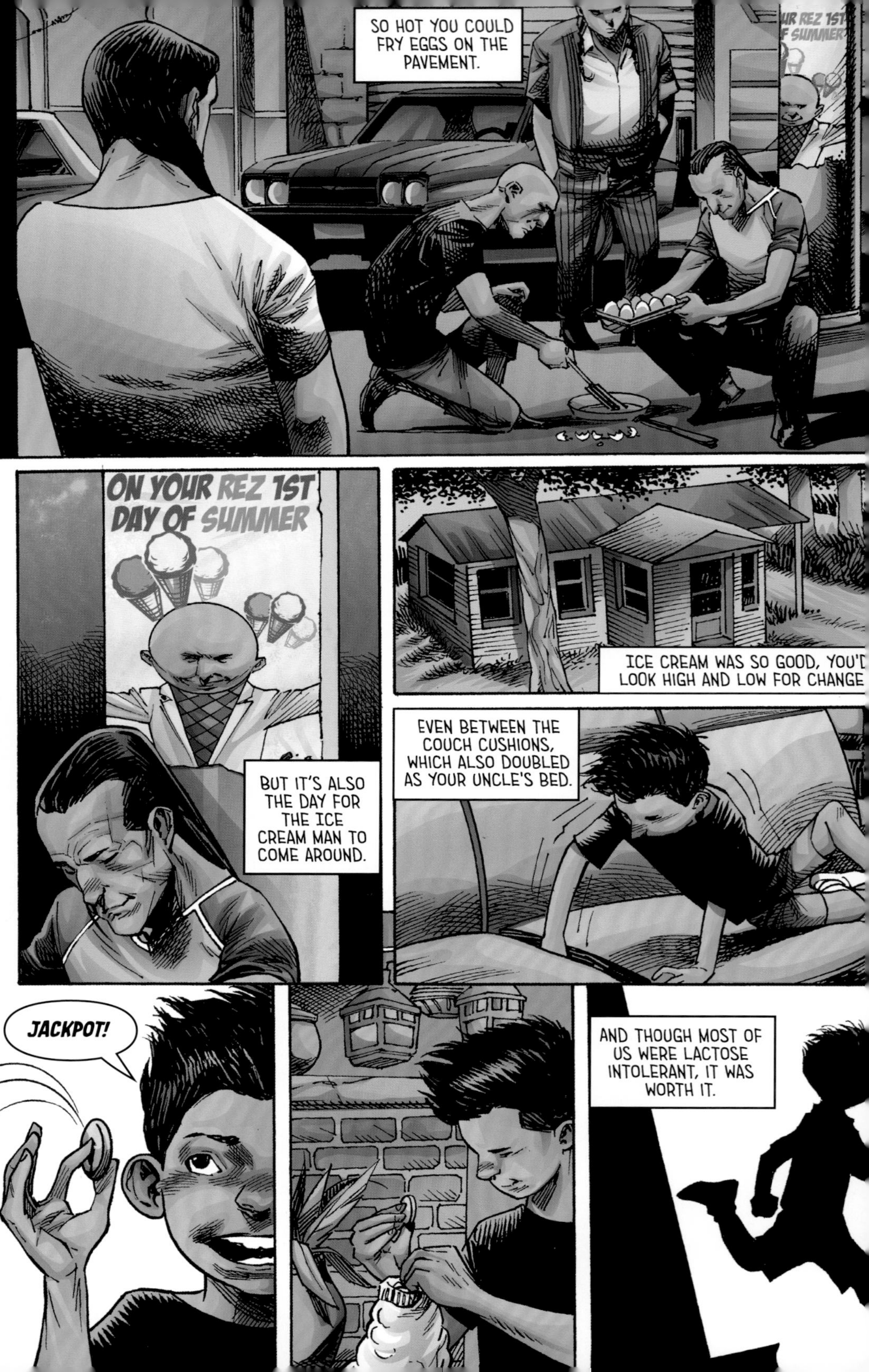
SO HOT YOU COULD FRY EGGS ON THE PAVEMENT.
UR REZ 1ST
F SUMMER
ON YOUR REZ 1ST DAY OF SUMMER
BUT IT'S ALSO THE DAY FOR THE ICE CREAM MAN TO COME AROUND.
ICE CREAM WAS SO GOOD, YOU'D LOOK HIGH AND LOW FOR CHANGE
EVEN BETWEEN THE COUCH CUSHIONS, WHICH ALSO DOUBLED AS YOUR UNCLE'S BED.
JACKPOT!
AND THOUGH MOST OF US WERE LACTOSE INTOLERANT, IT WAS WORTH IT.

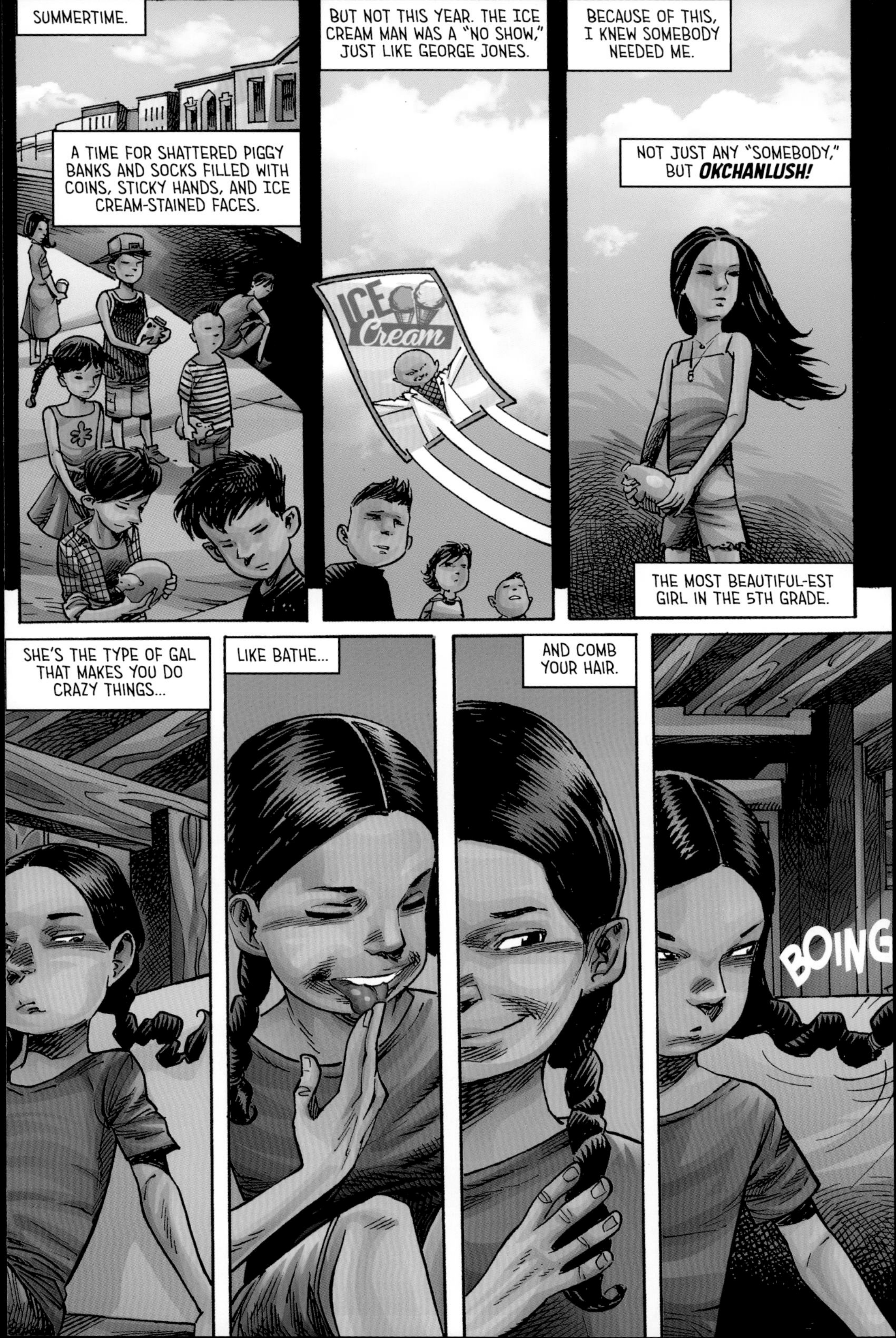
SUMMERTIME.
A TIME FOR SHATTERED PIGGY BANKS AND SOCKS FILLED WITH COINS, STICKY HANDS, AND ICE CREAM-STAINED FACES.
BUT NOT THIS YEAR. THE ICE CREAM MAN WAS A "NO SHOW," JUST LIKE GEORGE JONES.
ICE Cream
BECAUSE OF THIS, I KNEW SOMEBODY NEEDED ME.
NOT JUST ANY "SOMEBODY," BUT **OKCHANLUSH!**
THE MOST BEAUTIFUL-EST GIRL IN THE 5TH GRADE.
SHE'S THE TYPE OF GAL THAT MAKES YOU DO CRAZY THINGS...
LIKE BATHE...
AND COMB YOUR HAIR.
BOING

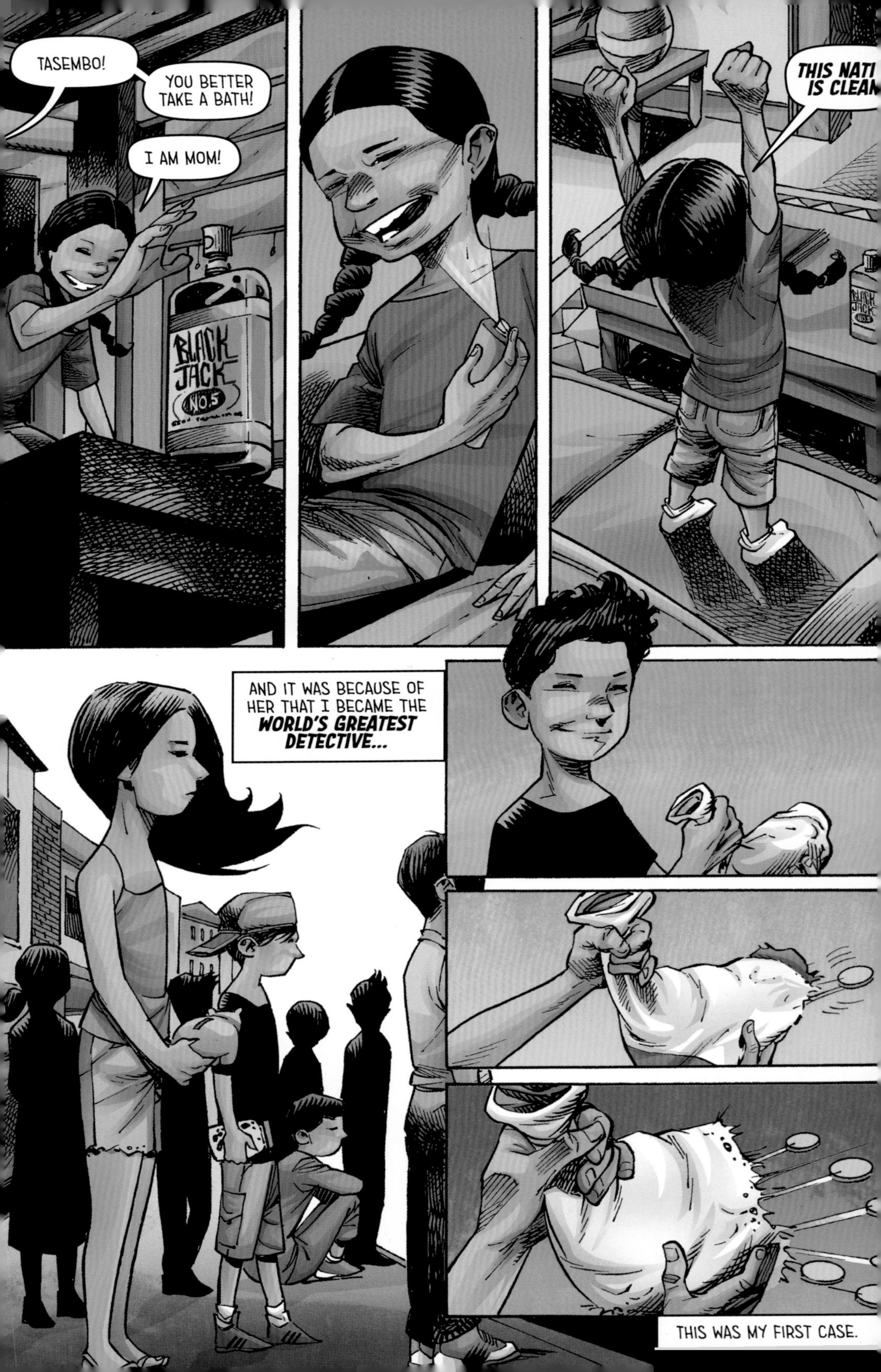
TASEMBO!
YOU BETTER TAKE A BATH!
I AM MOM!
BLACK JACK NO.5
THIS NATI IS CLEAN
AND IT WAS BECAUSE OF HER THAT I BECAME THE ***WORLD'S GREATEST DETECTIVE...***
THIS WAS MY FIRST CASE.

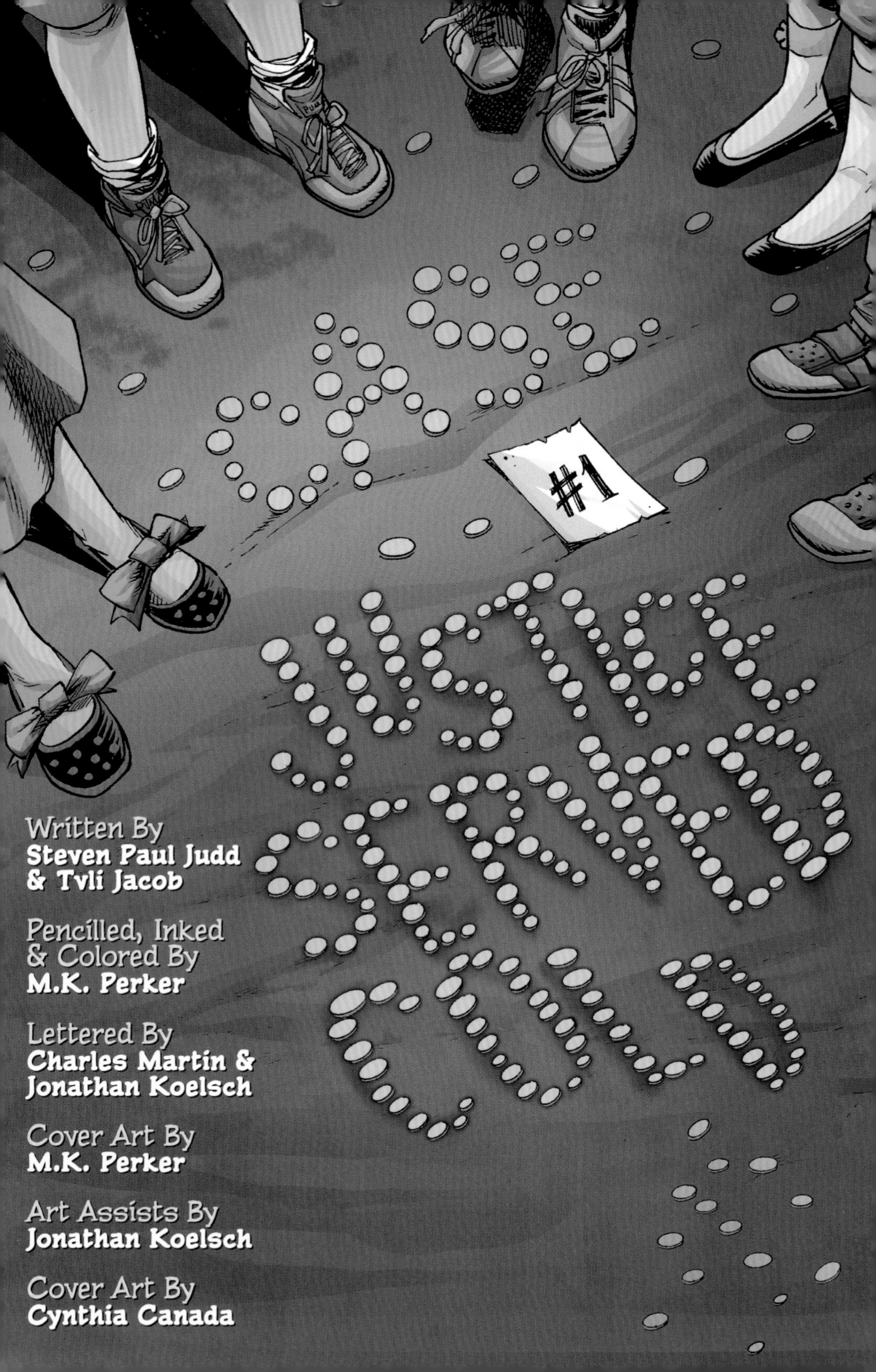
#1
JUSTICE
SERVED
COLD

Written By
Steven Paul Judd & Tvli Jacob

Pencilled, Inked & Colored By
M.K. Perker

Lettered By
Charles Martin & Jonathan Koelsch

Cover Art By
M.K. Perker

Art Assists By
Jonathan Koelsch

Cover Art By
Cynthia Canada

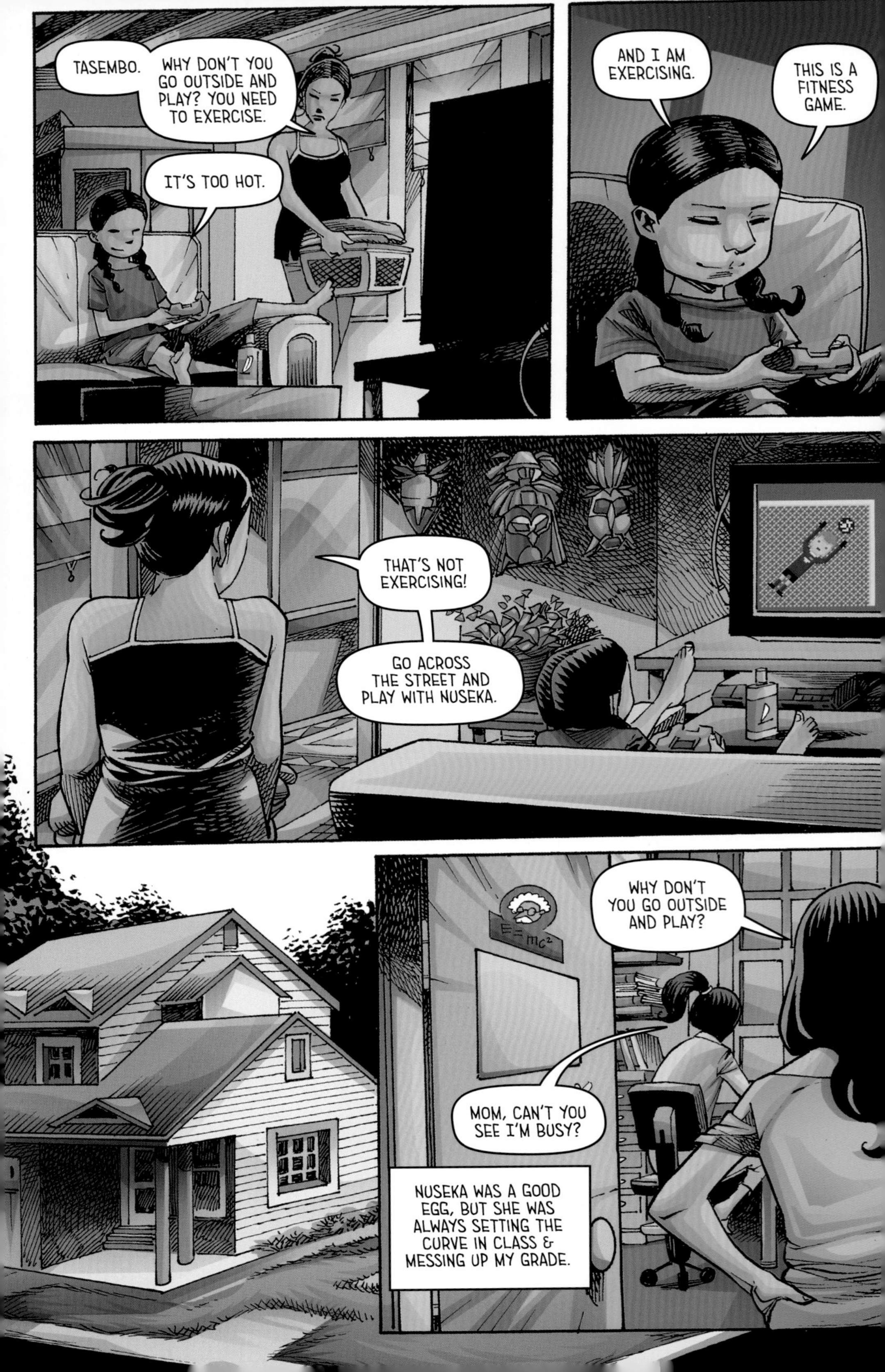
TASEMBO.
WHY DON'T YOU GO OUTSIDE AND PLAY? YOU NEED TO EXERCISE.
IT'S TOO HOT.
AND I AM EXERCISING.
THIS IS A FITNESS GAME.
THAT'S NOT EXERCISING!
GO ACROSS THE STREET AND PLAY WITH NUSEKA.
WHY DON'T YOU GO OUTSIDE AND PLAY?
MOM, CAN'T YOU SEE I'M BUSY?
NUSEKA WAS A GOOD EGG, BUT SHE WAS ALWAYS SETTING THE CURVE IN CLASS & MESSING UP MY GRADE.

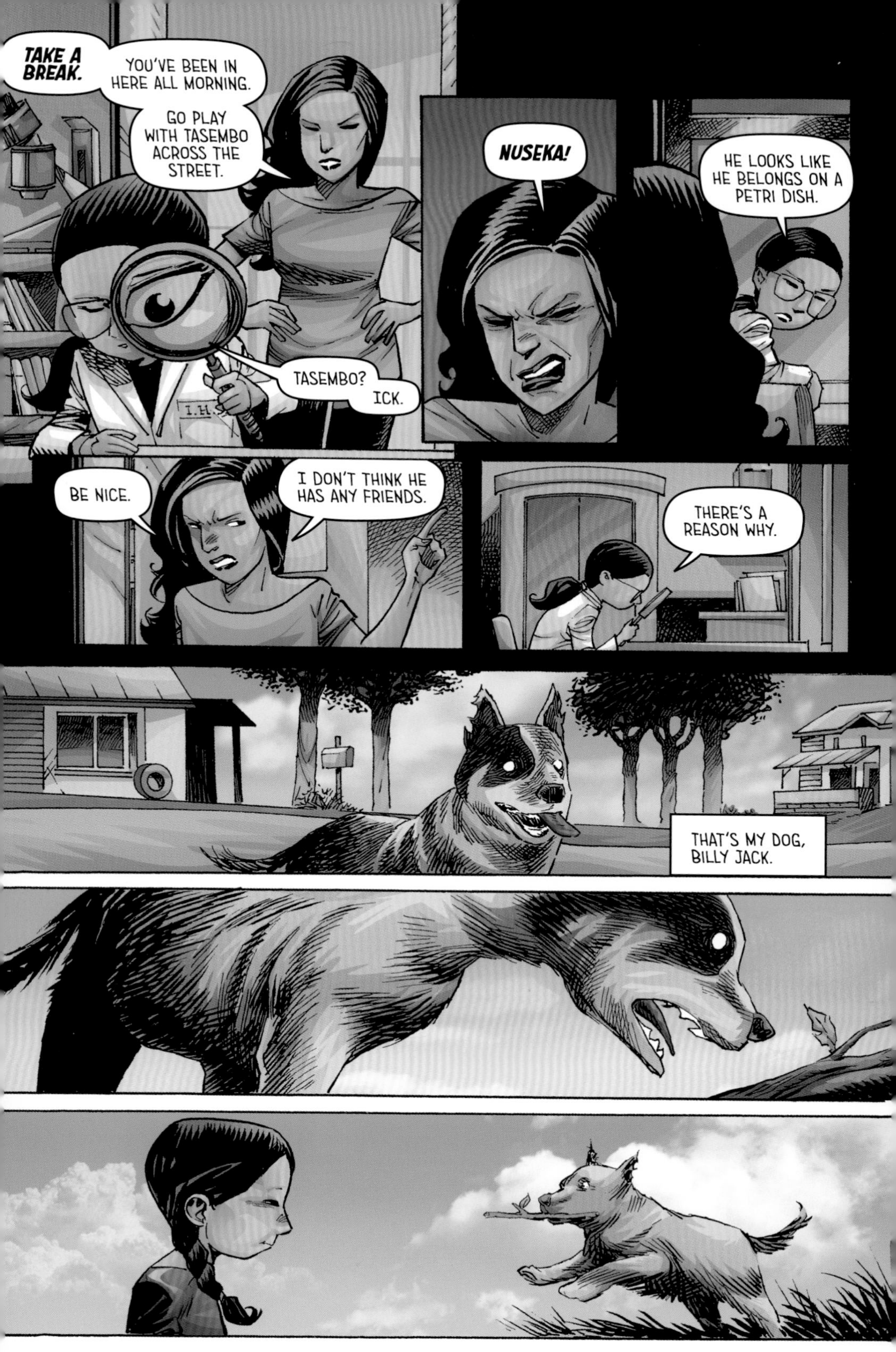
TAKE A BREAK.
YOU'VE BEEN IN HERE ALL MORNING.
GO PLAY WITH TASEMBO ACROSS THE STREET.
TASEMBO? ICK.
NUSEKA!
HE LOOKS LIKE HE BELONGS ON A PETRI DISH.
BE NICE.
I DON'T THINK HE HAS ANY FRIENDS.
THERE'S A REASON WHY.
THAT'S MY DOG, BILLY JACK.

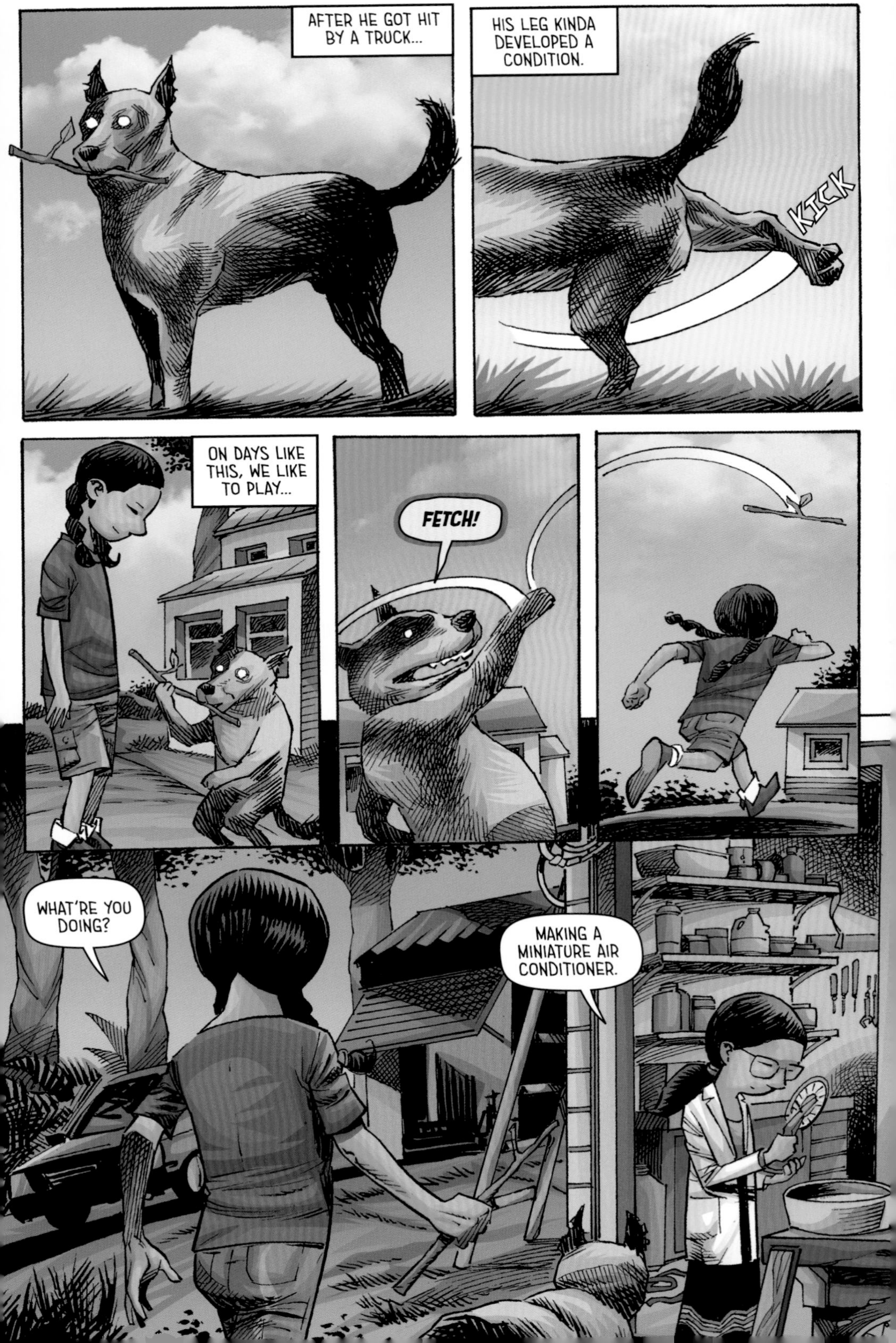
AFTER HE GOT HIT BY A TRUCK...
HIS LEG KINDA DEVELOPED A CONDITION.
KICK
ON DAYS LIKE THIS, WE LIKE TO PLAY...
FETCH!
WHAT'RE YOU DOING?
MAKING A MINIATURE AIR CONDITIONER.

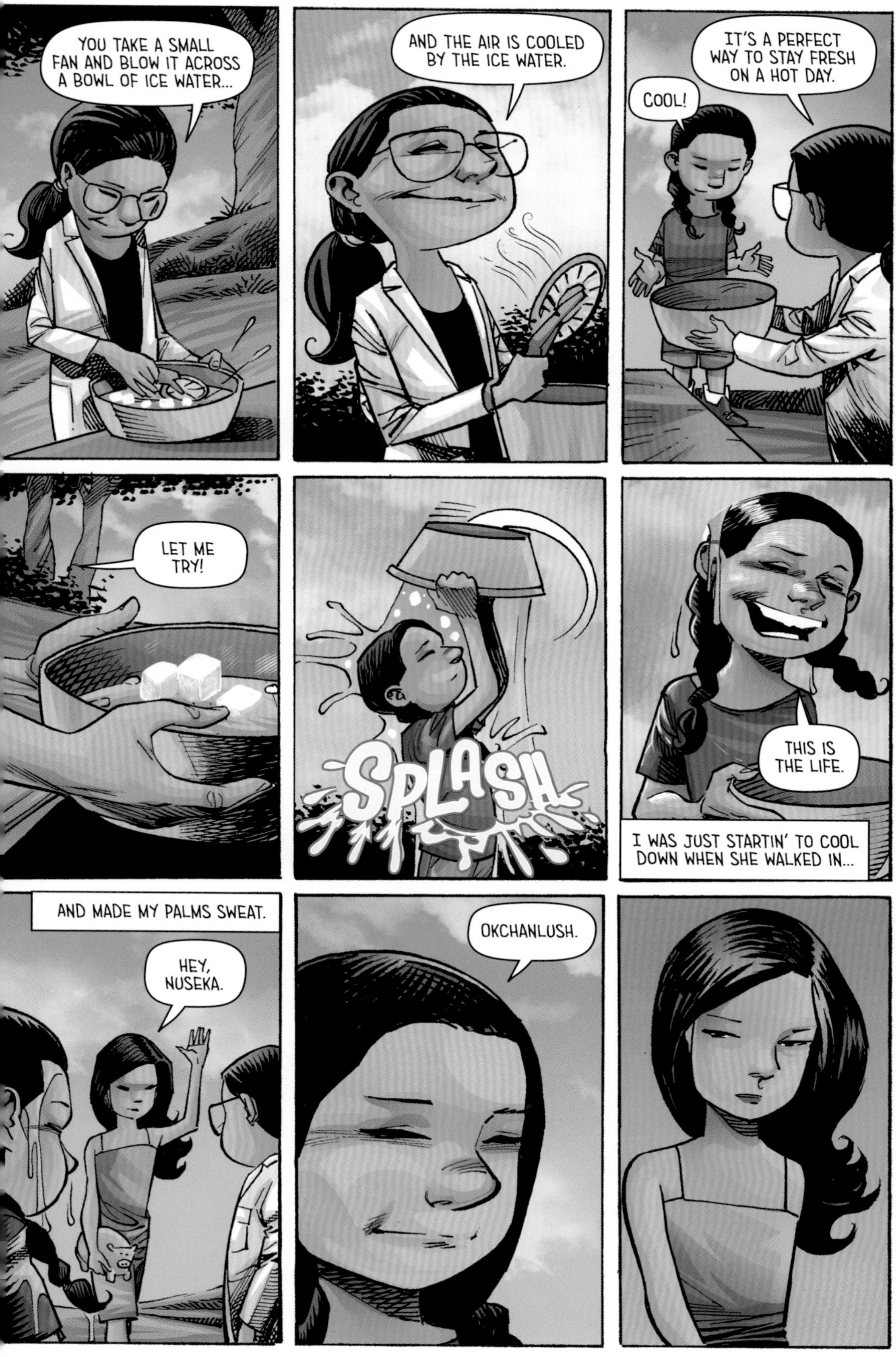

YOU TAKE A SMALL FAN AND BLOW IT ACROSS A BOWL OF ICE WATER...
AND THE AIR IS COOLED BY THE ICE WATER.
COOL!
IT'S A PERFECT WAY TO STAY FRESH ON A HOT DAY.
LET ME TRY!
SPLASH
THIS IS THE LIFE.
I WAS JUST STARTIN' TO COOL DOWN WHEN SHE WALKED IN...
AND MADE MY PALMS SWEAT.
HEY, NUSEKA.
OKCHANLUSH.

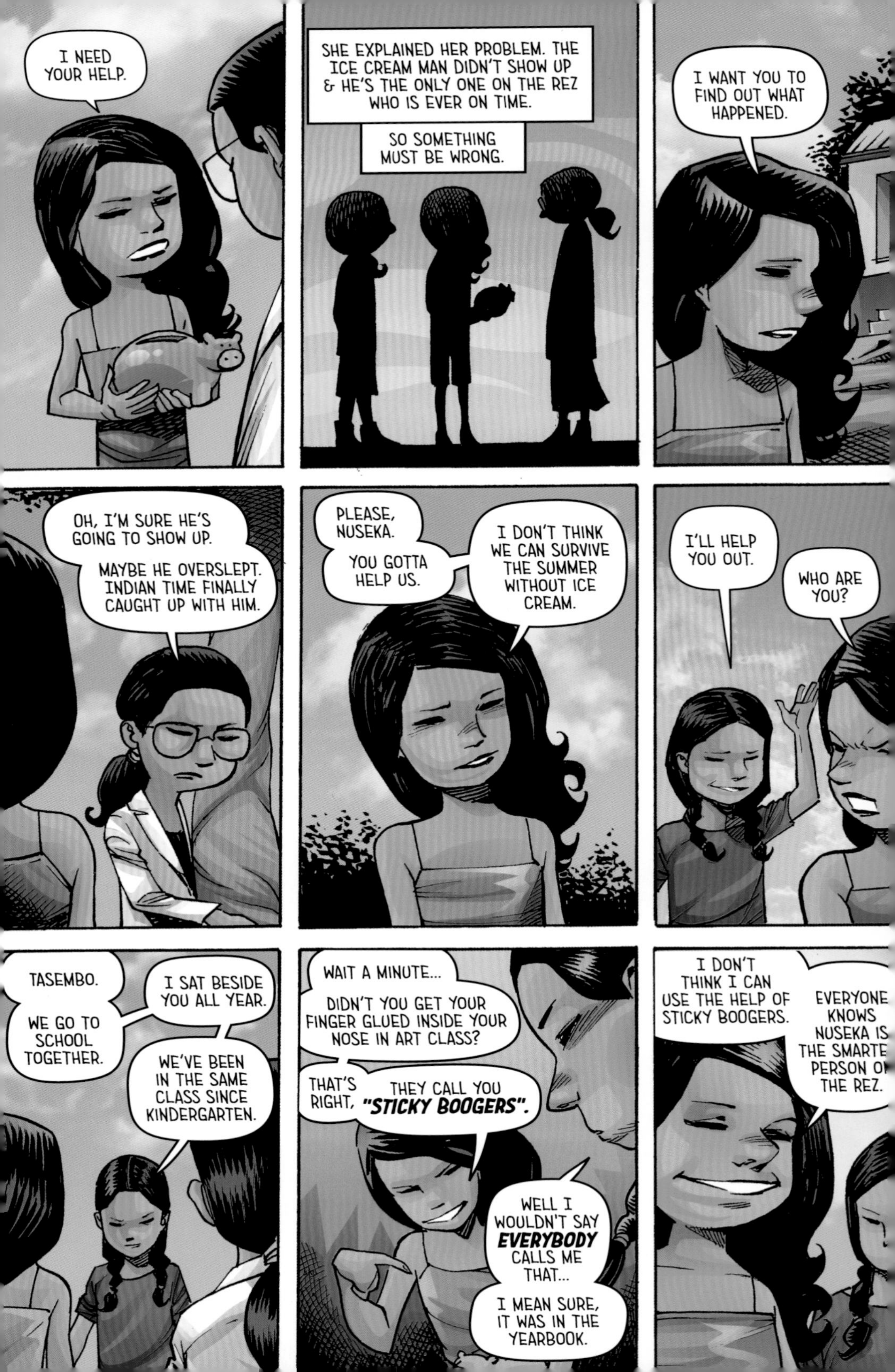
I NEED YOUR HELP.
SHE EXPLAINED HER PROBLEM. THE ICE CREAM MAN DIDN'T SHOW UP & HE'S THE ONLY ONE ON THE REZ WHO IS EVER ON TIME.
SO SOMETHING MUST BE WRONG.
I WANT YOU TO FIND OUT WHAT HAPPENED.
OH, I'M SURE HE'S GOING TO SHOW UP.
MAYBE HE OVERSLEPT. INDIAN TIME FINALLY CAUGHT UP WITH HIM.
PLEASE, NUSEKA.
YOU GOTTA HELP US.
I DON'T THINK WE CAN SURVIVE THE SUMMER WITHOUT ICE CREAM.
I'LL HELP YOU OUT.
WHO ARE YOU?
TASEMBO.
WE GO TO SCHOOL TOGETHER.
I SAT BESIDE YOU ALL YEAR.
WE'VE BEEN IN THE SAME CLASS SINCE KINDERGARTEN.
WAIT A MINUTE...
DIDN'T YOU GET YOUR FINGER GLUED INSIDE YOUR NOSE IN ART CLASS?
THAT'S RIGHT,
THEY CALL YOU "STICKY BOOGERS".
WELL I WOULDN'T SAY EVERYBODY CALLS ME THAT...
I MEAN SURE, IT WAS IN THE YEARBOOK.
I DON'T THINK I CAN USE THE HELP OF STICKY BOOGERS.

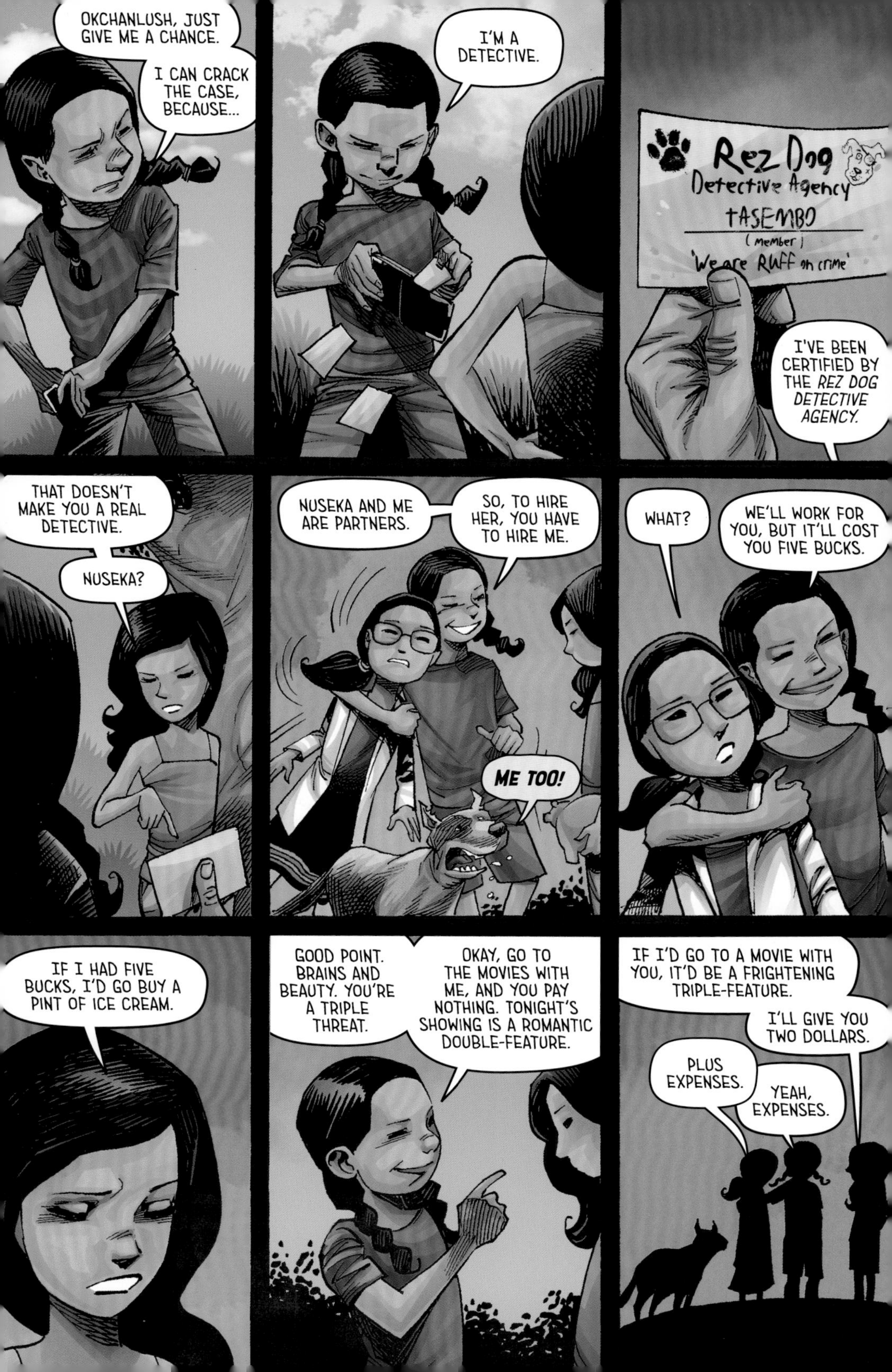
OKCHANLUSH, JUST GIVE ME A CHANCE.
I CAN CRACK THE CASE, BECAUSE...
I'M A DETECTIVE.
Rez Dog Detective Agency
TASEMBO
(member)
'We are RUFF on crime'
I'VE BEEN CERTIFIED BY THE *REZ DOG DETECTIVE AGENCY.*
THAT DOESN'T MAKE YOU A REAL DETECTIVE.
NUSEKA?
NUSEKA AND ME ARE PARTNERS.
SO, TO HIRE HER, YOU HAVE TO HIRE ME.
ME TOO!
WHAT?
WE'LL WORK FOR YOU, BUT IT'LL COST YOU FIVE BUCKS.
IF I HAD FIVE BUCKS, I'D GO BUY A PINT OF ICE CREAM.
GOOD POINT. BRAINS AND BEAUTY. YOU'RE A TRIPLE THREAT.
OKAY, GO TO THE MOVIES WITH ME, AND YOU PAY NOTHING. TONIGHT'S SHOWING IS A ROMANTIC DOUBLE-FEATURE.
IF I'D GO TO A MOVIE WITH YOU, IT'D BE A FRIGHTENING TRIPLE-FEATURE.
I'LL GIVE YOU TWO DOLLARS.
PLUS EXPENSES.
YEAH, EXPENSES.

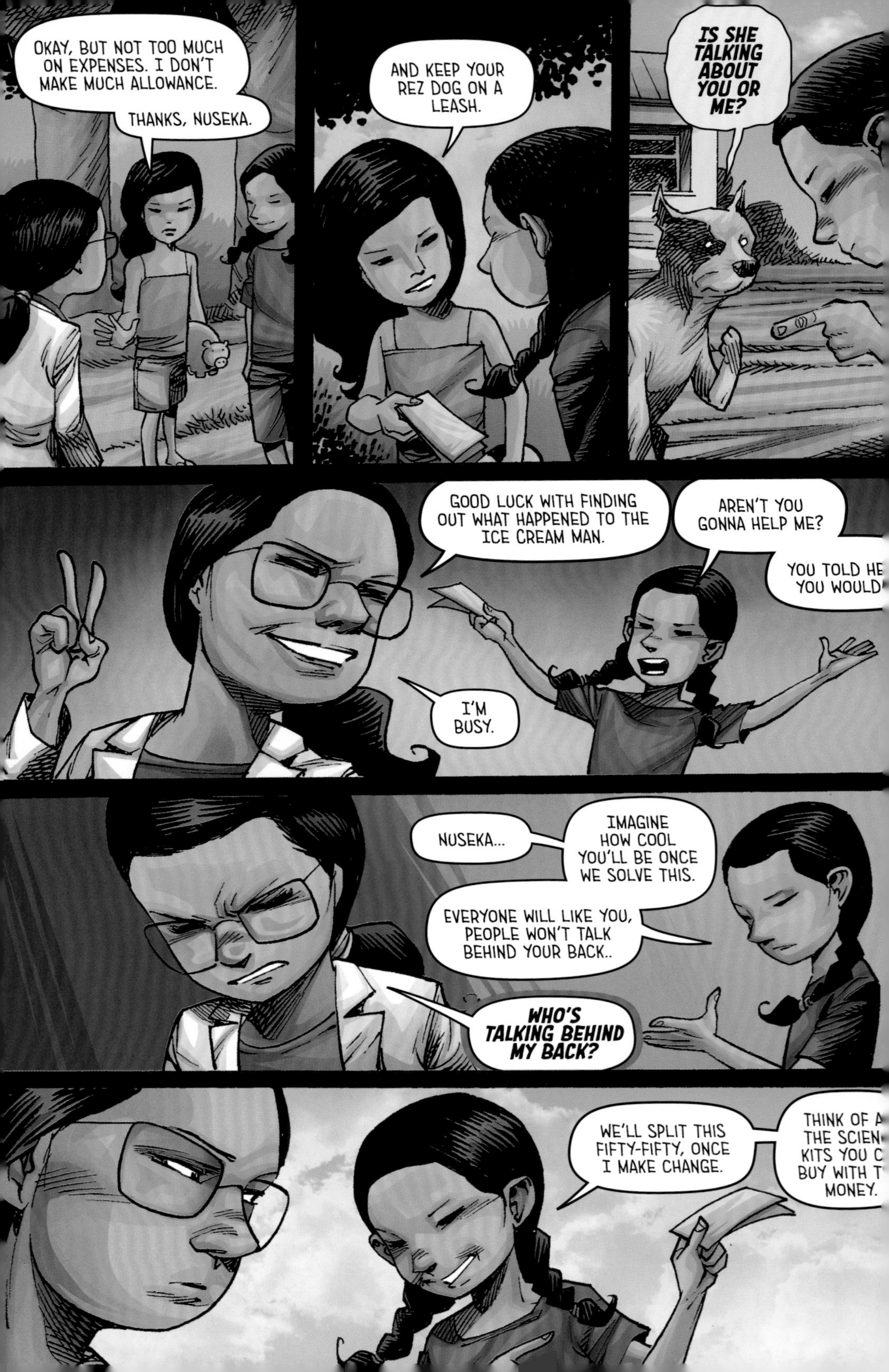
OKAY, BUT NOT TOO MUCH ON EXPENSES. I DON'T MAKE MUCH ALLOWANCE.
THANKS, NUSEKA.
AND KEEP YOUR REZ DOG ON A LEASH.
IS SHE TALKING ABOUT YOU OR ME?
GOOD LUCK WITH FINDING OUT WHAT HAPPENED TO THE ICE CREAM MAN.
AREN'T YOU GONNA HELP ME?
YOU TOLD HE YOU WOULD
I'M BUSY.
NUSEKA...
IMAGINE HOW COOL YOU'LL BE ONCE WE SOLVE THIS.
EVERYONE WILL LIKE YOU, PEOPLE WON'T TALK BEHIND YOUR BACK..
WHO'S TALKING BEHIND MY BACK?
WE'LL SPLIT THIS FIFTY-FIFTY, ONCE I MAKE CHANGE.
THINK OF A THE SCIEN KITS YOU C BUY WITH T MONEY.

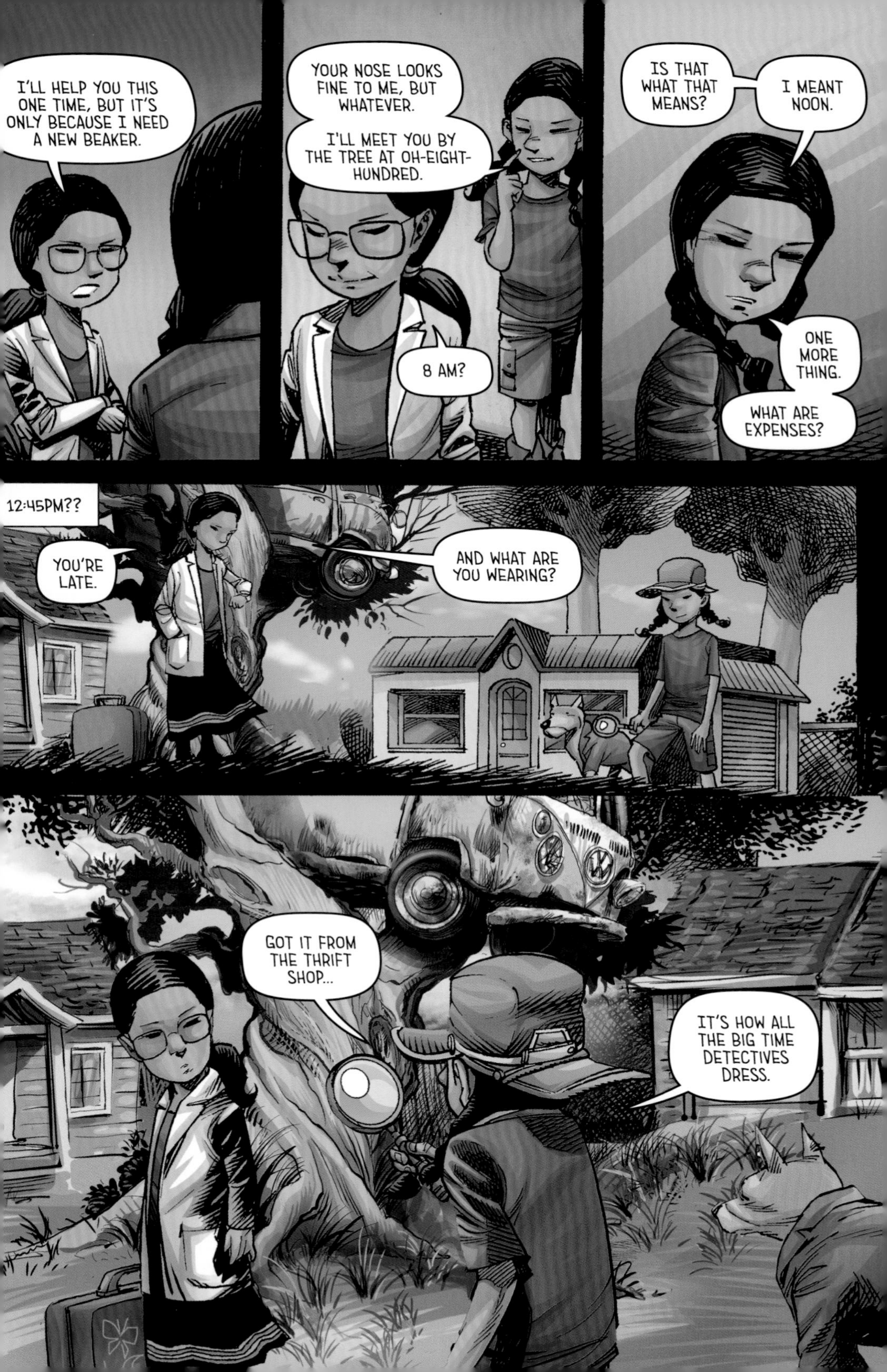
I'LL HELP YOU THIS ONE TIME, BUT IT'S ONLY BECAUSE I NEED A NEW BEAKER.
YOUR NOSE LOOKS FINE TO ME, BUT WHATEVER.
I'LL MEET YOU BY THE TREE AT OH-EIGHT-HUNDRED.
8 AM?
IS THAT WHAT THAT MEANS?
I MEANT NOON.
ONE MORE THING.
WHAT ARE EXPENSES?
12:45PM??
YOU'RE LATE.
AND WHAT ARE YOU WEARING?
GOT IT FROM THE THRIFT SHOP...
IT'S HOW ALL THE BIG TIME DETECTIVES DRESS.

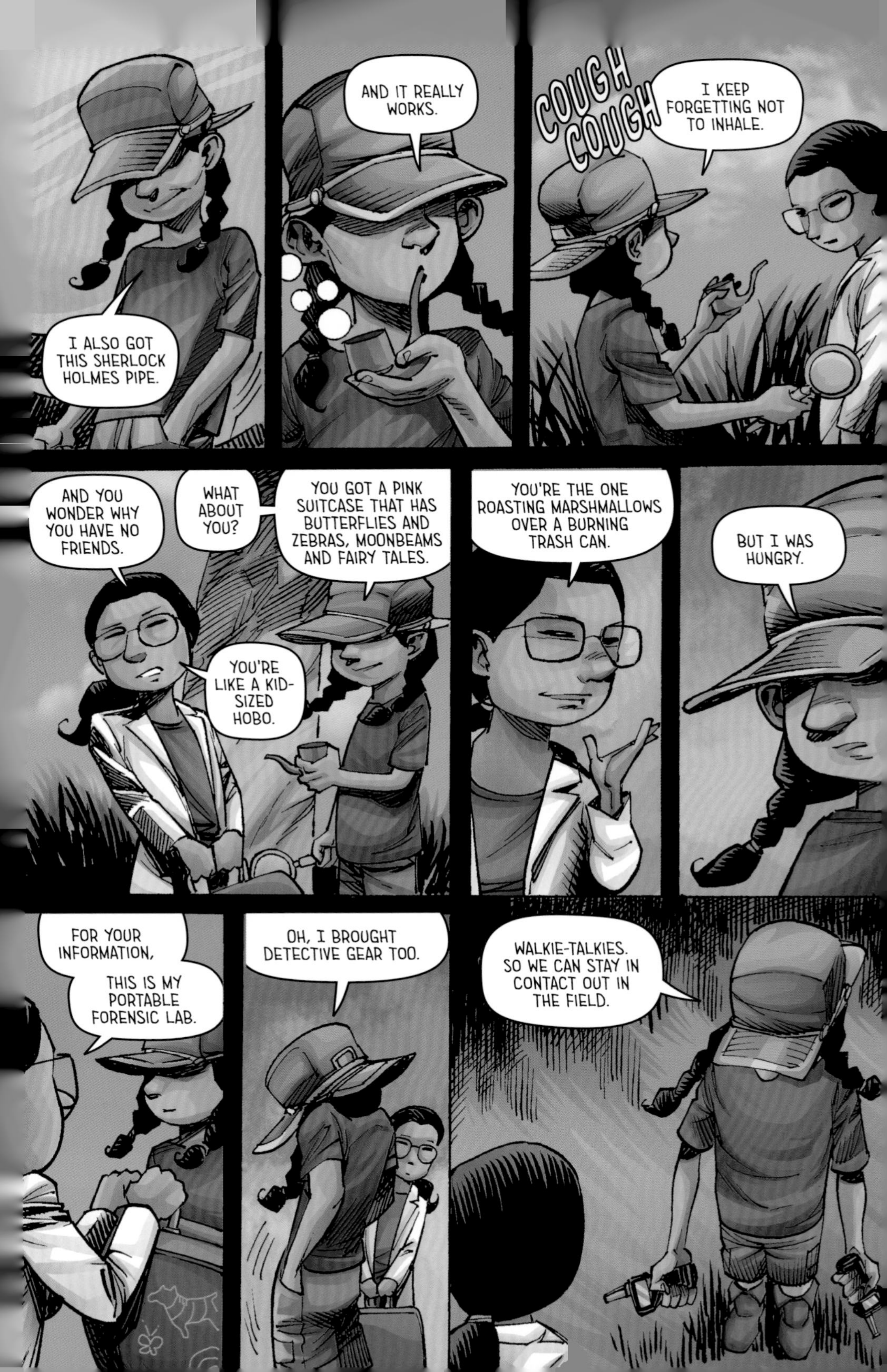
I ALSO GOT THIS SHERLOCK HOLMES PIPE.
AND IT REALLY WORKS.
COUGH COUGH
I KEEP FORGETTING NOT TO INHALE.
AND YOU WONDER WHY YOU HAVE NO FRIENDS.
WHAT ABOUT YOU?
YOU GOT A PINK SUITCASE THAT HAS BUTTERFLIES AND ZEBRAS, MOONBEAMS AND FAIRY TALES.
YOU'RE LIKE A KID-SIZED HOBO.
YOU'RE THE ONE ROASTING MARSHMALLOWS OVER A BURNING TRASH CAN.
BUT I WAS HUNGRY.
FOR YOUR INFORMATION,
THIS IS MY PORTABLE FORENSIC LAB.
OH, I BROUGHT DETECTIVE GEAR TOO.
WALKIE-TALKIES. SO WE CAN STAY IN CONTACT OUT IN THE FIELD.

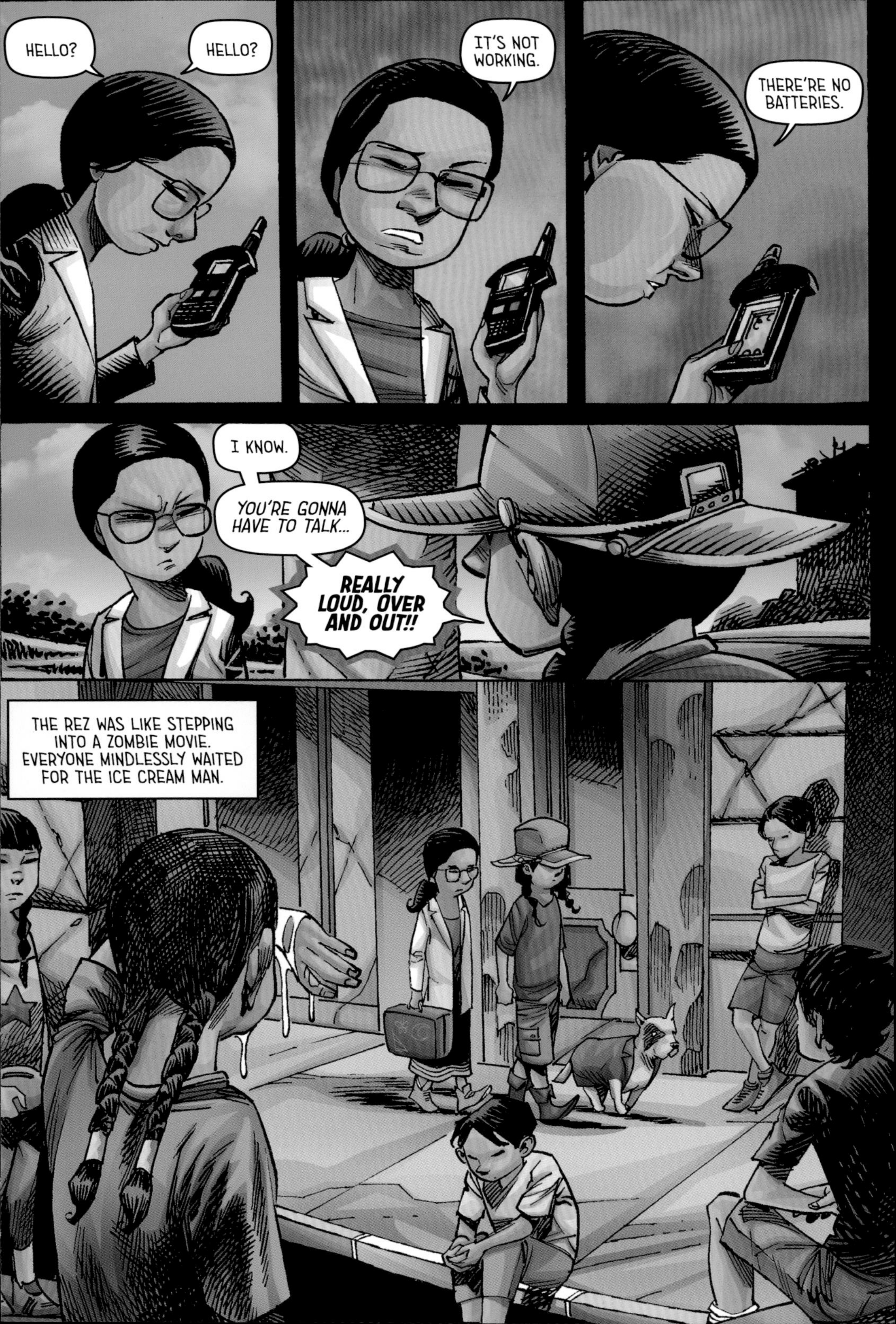
HELLO?
HELLO?
IT'S NOT WORKING.
THERE'RE NO BATTERIES.
I KNOW.
YOU'RE GONNA HAVE TO TALK...
REALLY LOUD, OVER AND OUT!!
THE REZ WAS LIKE STEPPING INTO A ZOMBIE MOVIE. EVERYONE MINDLESSLY WAITED FOR THE ICE CREAM MAN.

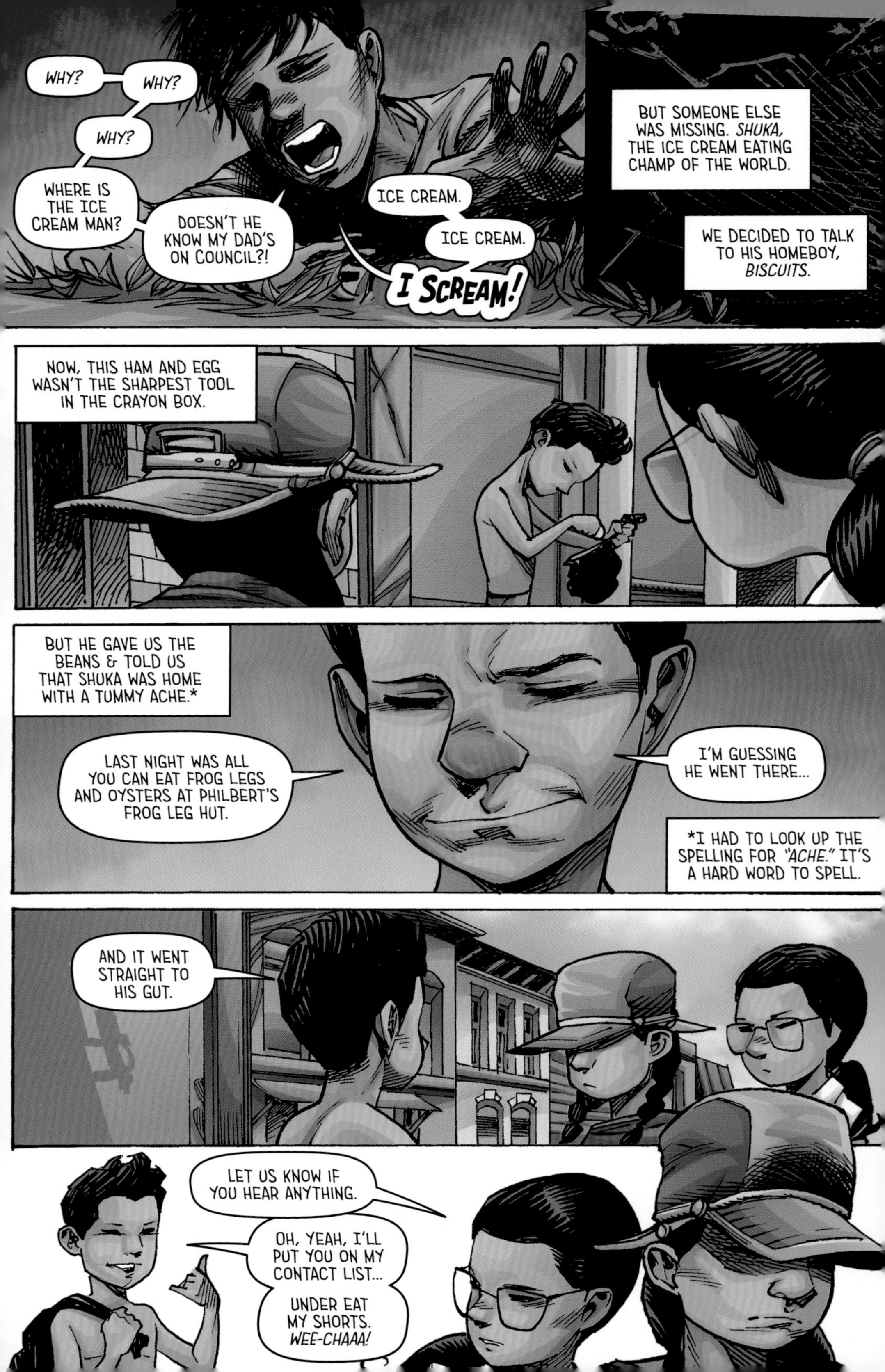
WHY?
WHY?
WHY?
WHERE IS THE ICE CREAM MAN?
DOESN'T HE KNOW MY DAD'S ON COUNCIL?!
ICE CREAM.
ICE CREAM.
I SCREAM!
BUT SOMEONE ELSE WAS MISSING. *SHUKA,* THE ICE CREAM EATING CHAMP OF THE WORLD.
WE DECIDED TO TALK TO HIS HOMEBOY, *BISCUITS.*
NOW, THIS HAM AND EGG WASN'T THE SHARPEST TOOL IN THE CRAYON BOX.
BUT HE GAVE US THE BEANS & TOLD US THAT SHUKA WAS HOME WITH A TUMMY ACHE.*
LAST NIGHT WAS ALL YOU CAN EAT FROG LEGS AND OYSTERS AT PHILBERT'S FROG LEG HUT.
I'M GUESSING HE WENT THERE...
*I HAD TO LOOK UP THE SPELLING FOR *"ACHE."* IT'S A HARD WORD TO SPELL.
AND IT WENT STRAIGHT TO HIS GUT.
LET US KNOW IF YOU HEAR ANYTHING.
OH, YEAH, I'LL PUT YOU ON MY CONTACT LIST...
UNDER EAT MY SHORTS. *WEE-CHAAA!*

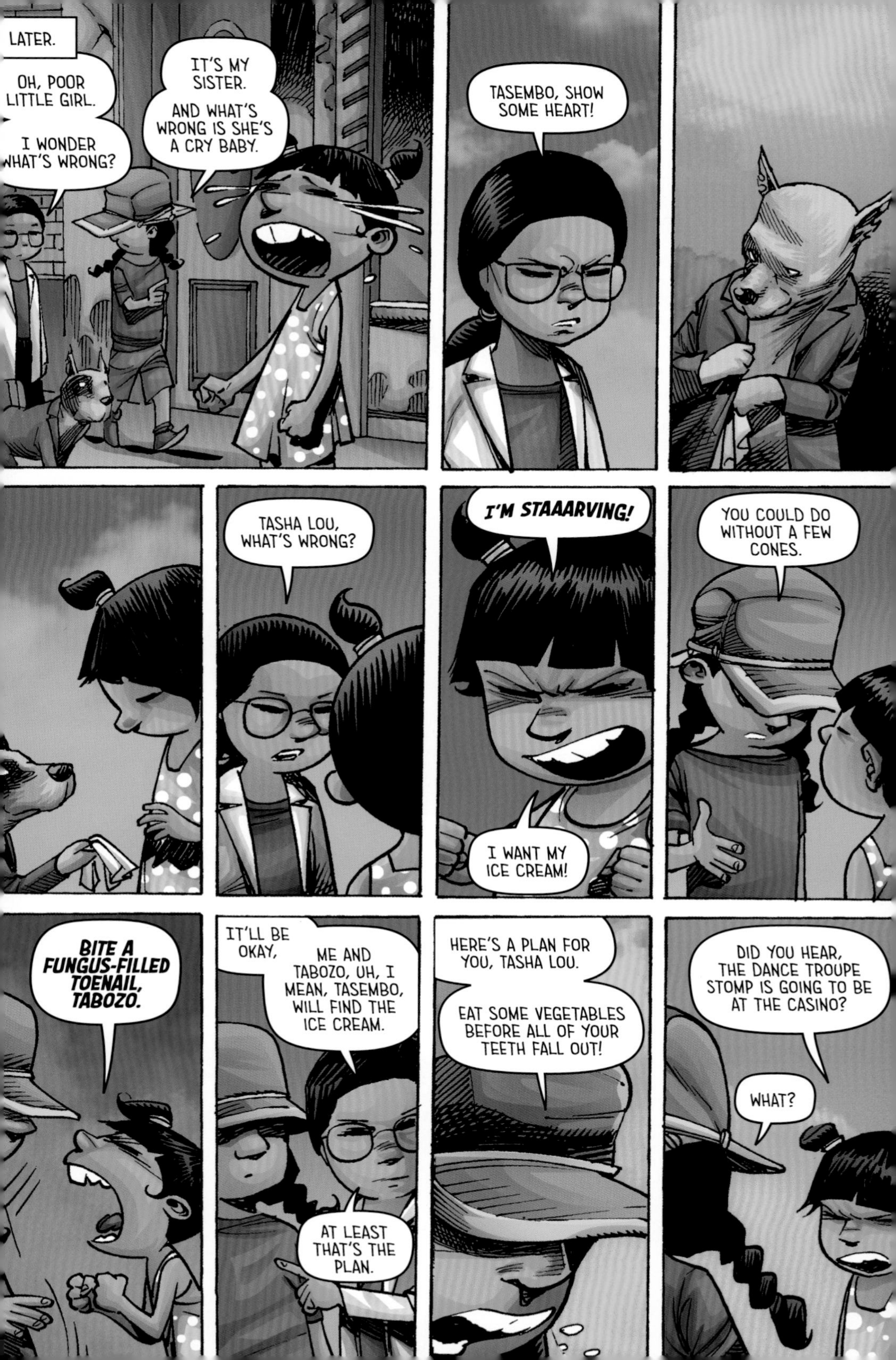

LATER.
OH, POOR LITTLE GIRL.
I WONDER WHAT'S WRONG?
IT'S MY SISTER.
AND WHAT'S WRONG IS SHE'S A CRY BABY.
TASEMBO, SHOW SOME HEART!
TASHA LOU, WHAT'S WRONG?
I'M STAAARVING!
I WANT MY ICE CREAM!
YOU COULD DO WITHOUT A FEW CONES.
BITE A FUNGUS-FILLED TOENAIL, TABOZO.
IT'LL BE OKAY,
ME AND TABOZO, UH, I MEAN, TASEMBO, WILL FIND THE ICE CREAM.
AT LEAST THAT'S THE PLAN.
HERE'S A PLAN FOR YOU, TASHA LOU.
EAT SOME VEGETABLES BEFORE ALL OF YOUR TEETH FALL OUT!
DID YOU HEAR, THE DANCE TROUPE STOMP IS GOING TO BE AT THE CASINO?
WHAT?

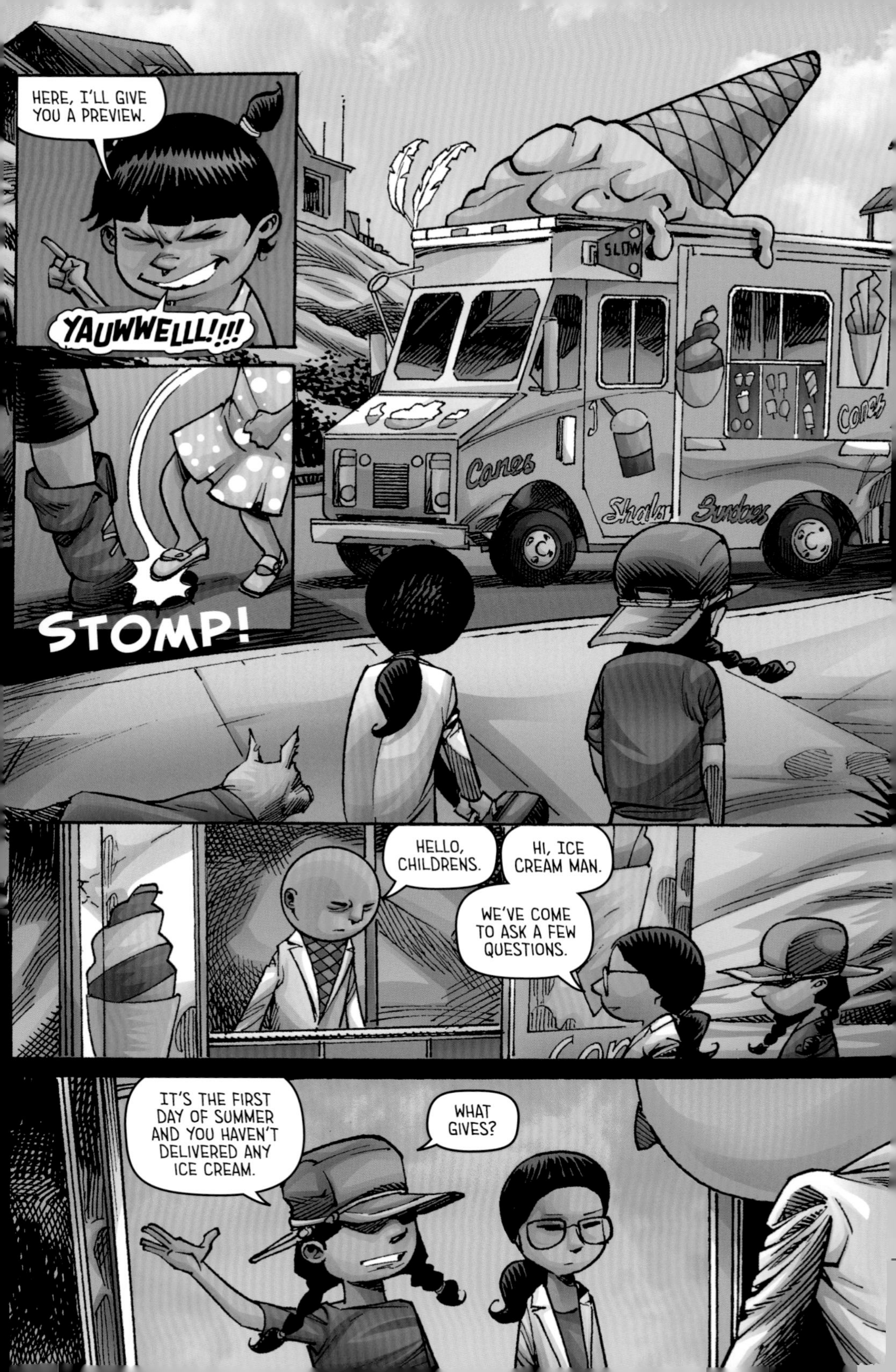
HERE, I'LL GIVE YOU A PREVIEW.
YAUWWELLL!!!!
STOMP!
SLOW
Cones
Shakes
Sundaes
Cones
HELLO, CHILDRENS.
HI, ICE CREAM MAN.
WE'VE COME TO ASK A FEW QUESTIONS.
IT'S THE FIRST DAY OF SUMMER AND YOU HAVEN'T DELIVERED ANY ICE CREAM.
WHAT GIVES?

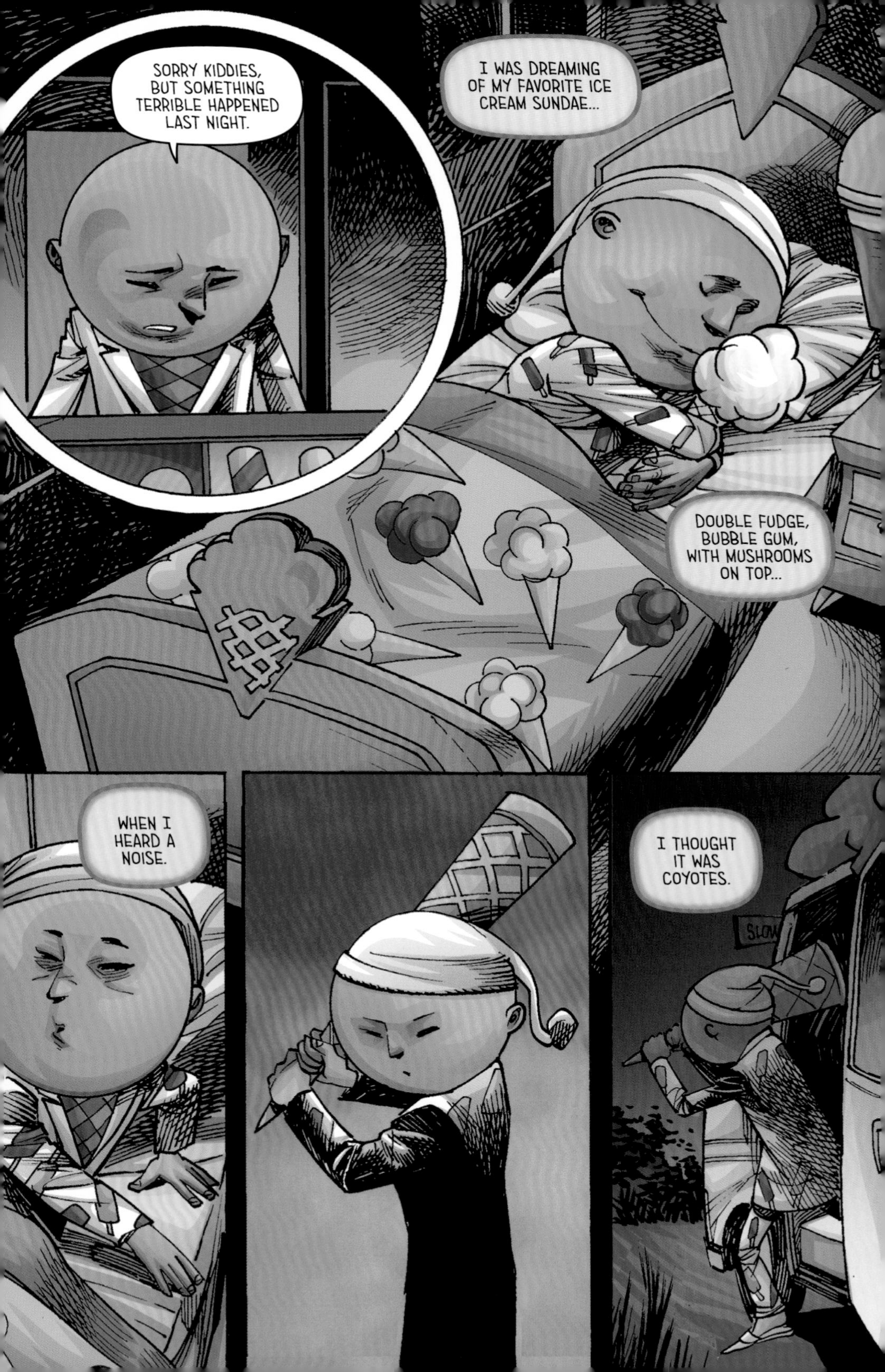
SORRY KIDDIES, BUT SOMETHING TERRIBLE HAPPENED LAST NIGHT.
I WAS DREAMING OF MY FAVORITE ICE CREAM SUNDAE...
DOUBLE FUDGE, BUBBLE GUM, WITH MUSHROOMS ON TOP...
WHEN I HEARD A NOISE.
I THOUGHT IT WAS COYOTES.
SLOW

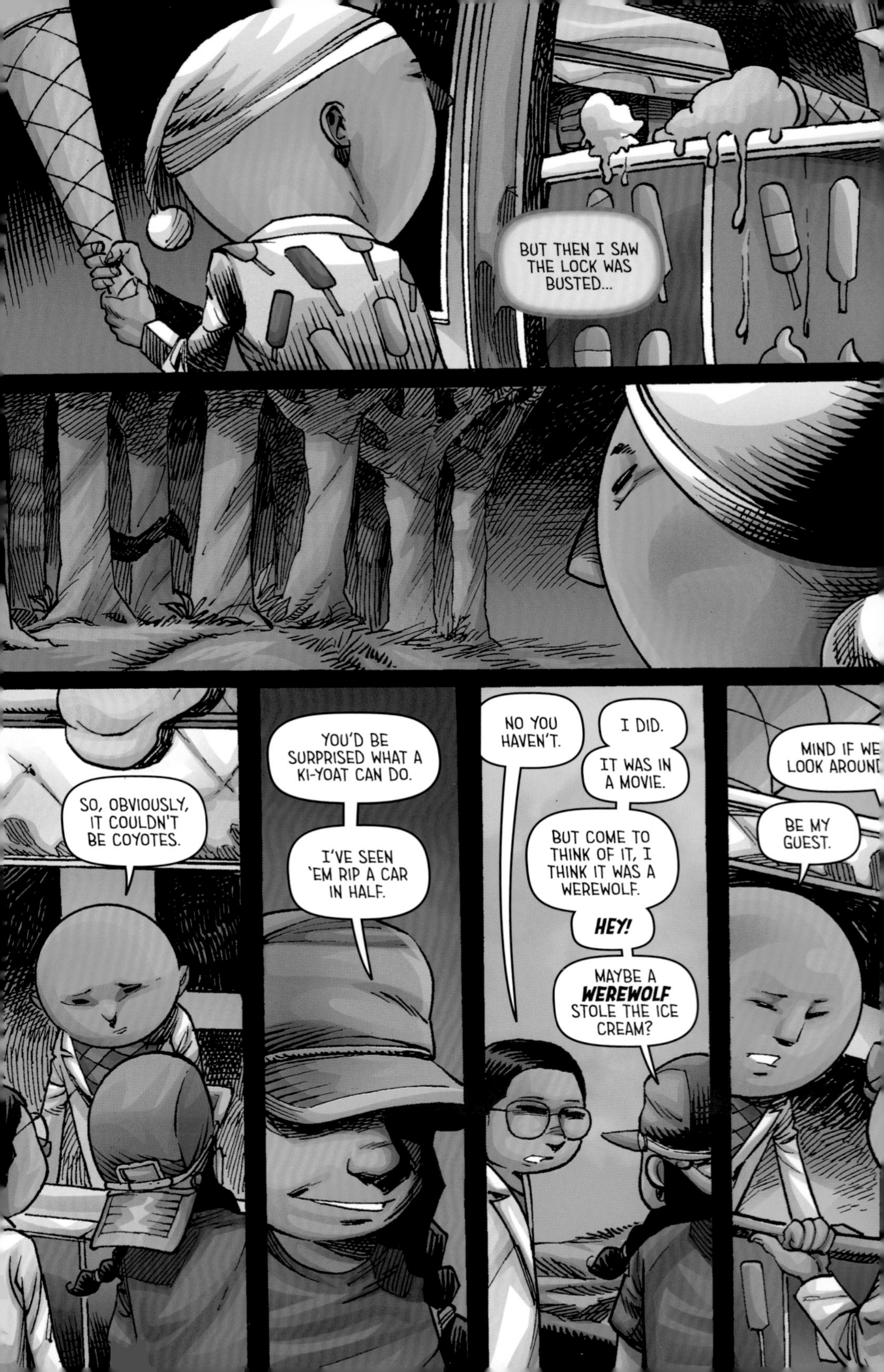
BUT THEN I SAW THE LOCK WAS BUSTED...
SO, OBVIOUSLY, IT COULDN'T BE COYOTES.
YOU'D BE SURPRISED WHAT A KI-YOAT CAN DO.
I'VE SEEN 'EM RIP A CAR IN HALF.
NO YOU HAVEN'T.
I DID.
IT WAS IN A MOVIE.
BUT COME TO THINK OF IT, I THINK IT WAS A WEREWOLF.
HEY!
MAYBE A WEREWOLF STOLE THE ICE CREAM?
MIND IF WE LOOK AROUND
BE MY GUEST.

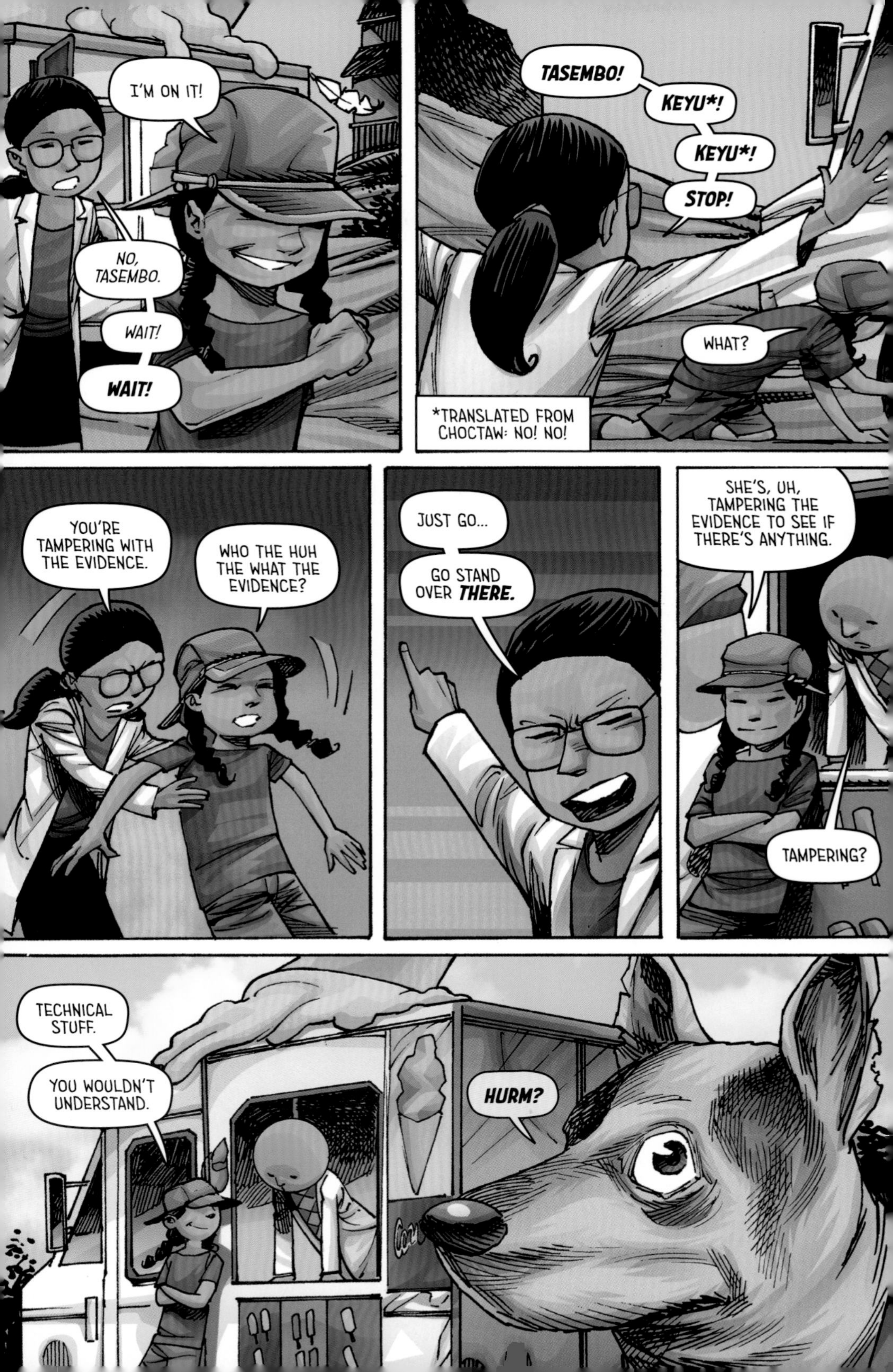

I'M ON IT!
NO, TASEMBO.
WAIT!
WAIT!
TASEMBO!
KEYU*!
KEYU*!
STOP!
WHAT?
*TRANSLATED FROM CHOCTAW: NO! NO!
YOU'RE TAMPERING WITH THE EVIDENCE.
WHO THE HUH THE WHAT THE EVIDENCE?
JUST GO...
GO STAND OVER THERE.
SHE'S, UH, TAMPERING THE EVIDENCE TO SEE IF THERE'S ANYTHING.
TAMPERING?
TECHNICAL STUFF.
YOU WOULDN'T UNDERSTAND.
HURM?

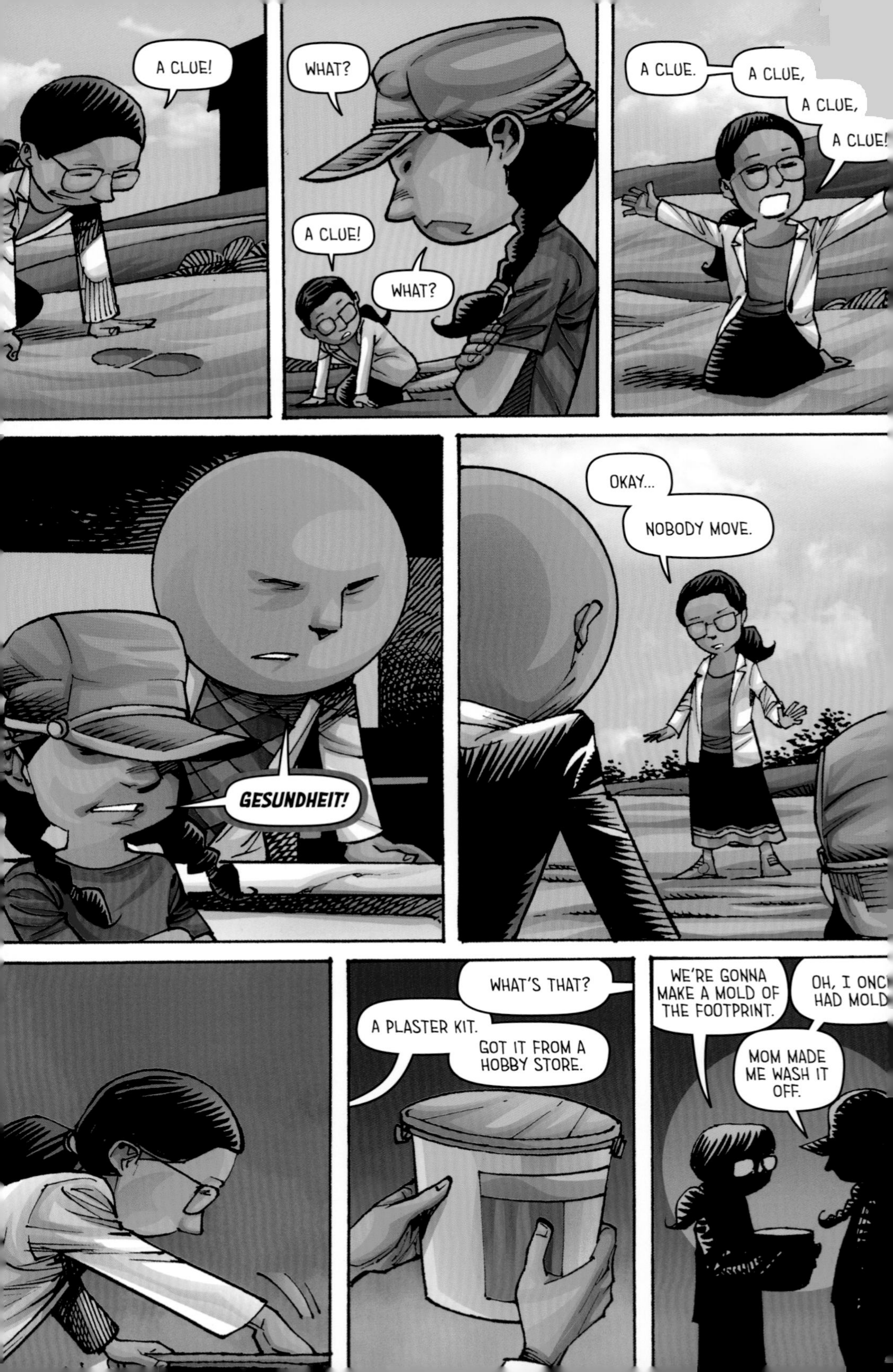
A CLUE!
WHAT?
A CLUE!
WHAT?
A CLUE.
A CLUE,
A CLUE,
A CLUE!
GESUNDHEIT!
OKAY...
NOBODY MOVE.
WHAT'S THAT?
A PLASTER KIT.
GOT IT FROM A HOBBY STORE.
WE'RE GONNA MAKE A MOLD OF THE FOOTPRINT.
OH, I ONC
HAD MOLD
MOM MADE ME WASH IT OFF.

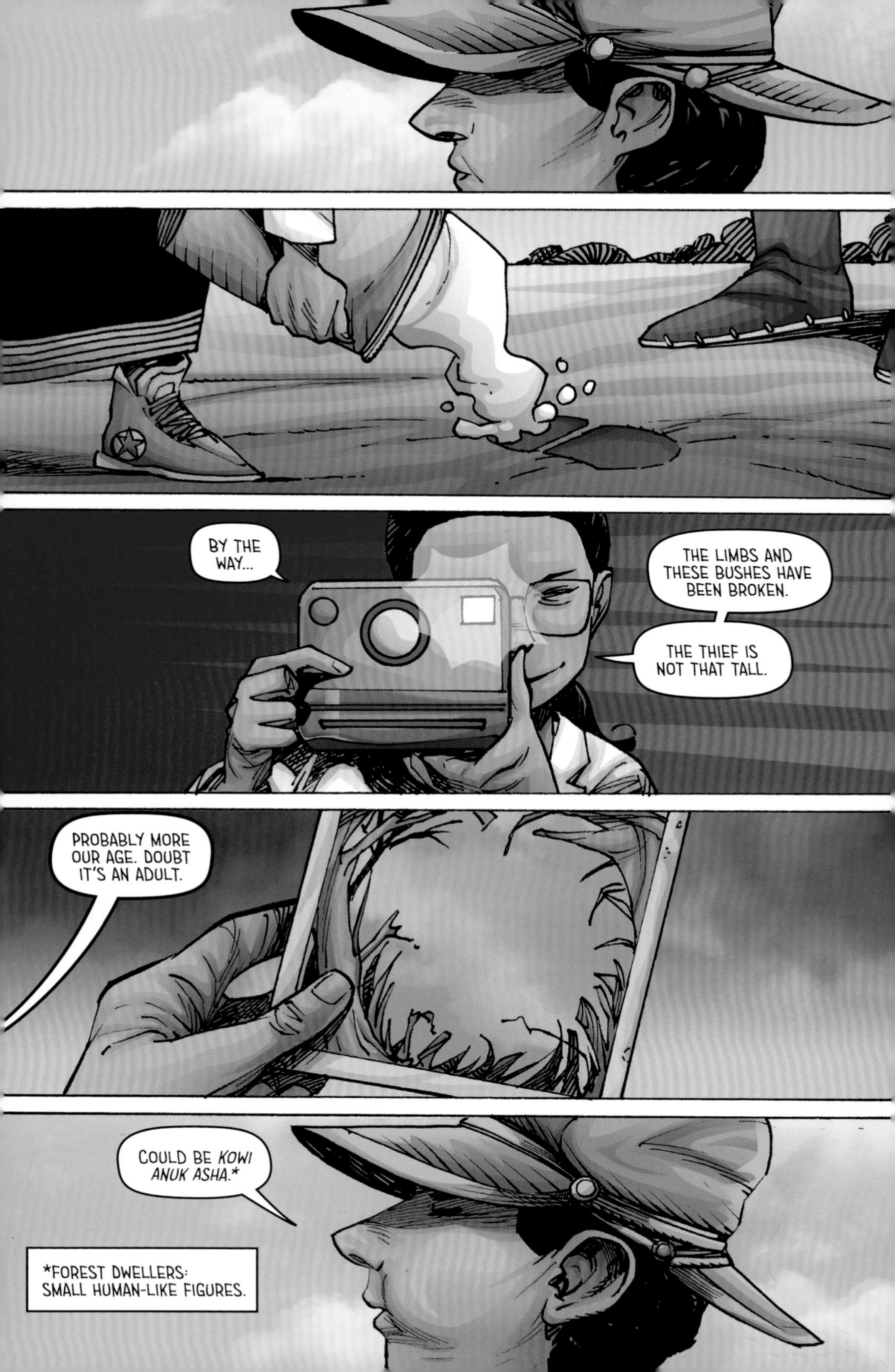
BY THE WAY...
THE LIMBS AND THESE BUSHES HAVE BEEN BROKEN.
THE THIEF IS NOT THAT TALL.
PROBABLY MORE OUR AGE. DOUBT IT'S AN ADULT.
COULD BE *KOWI ANUK ASHA.**
*FOREST DWELLERS: SMALL HUMAN-LIKE FIGURES.

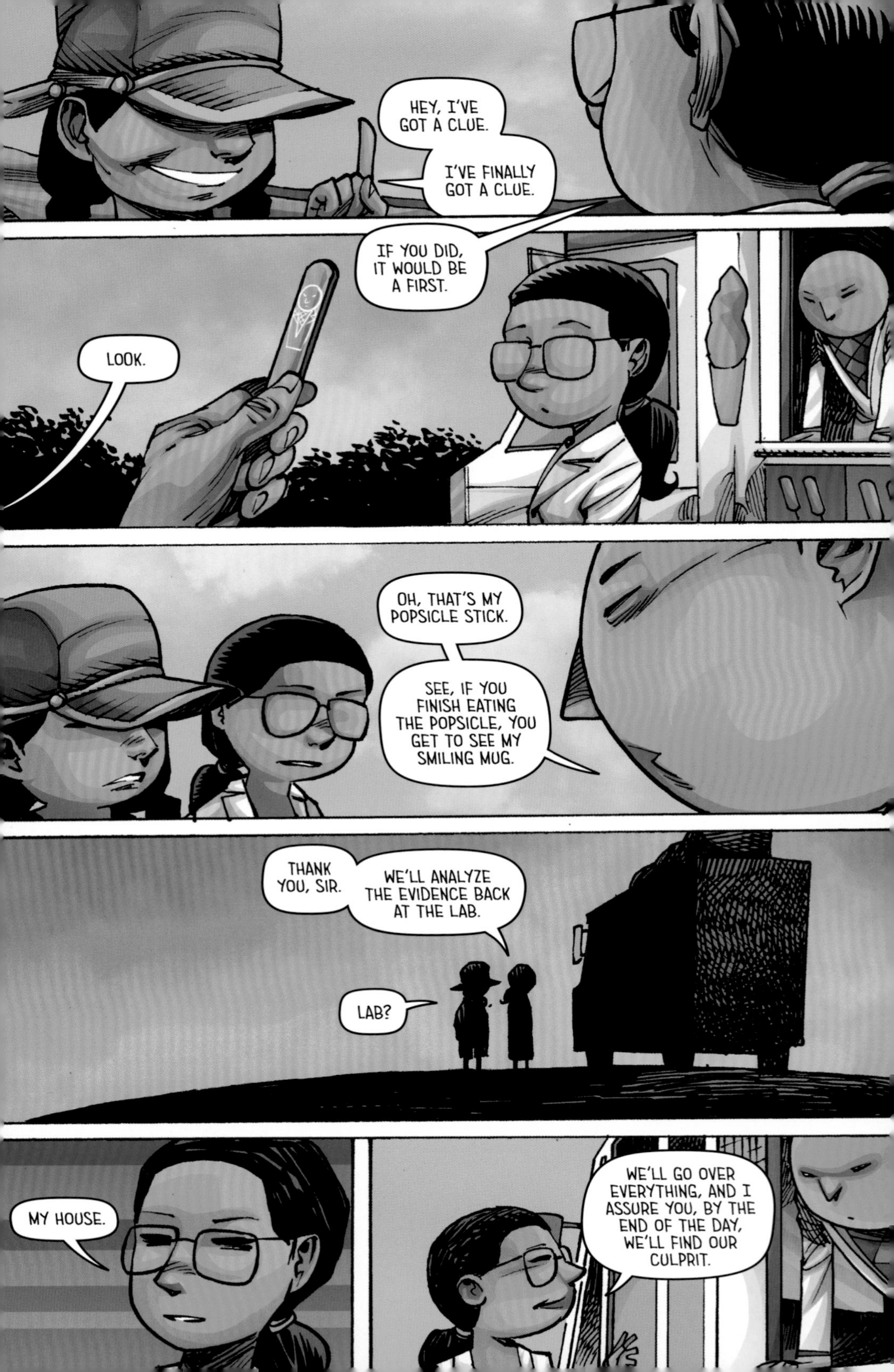
HEY, I'VE GOT A CLUE.
I'VE FINALLY GOT A CLUE.
IF YOU DID, IT WOULD BE A FIRST.
LOOK.
OH, THAT'S MY POPSICLE STICK.
SEE, IF YOU FINISH EATING THE POPSICLE, YOU GET TO SEE MY SMILING MUG.
THANK YOU, SIR.
WE'LL ANALYZE THE EVIDENCE BACK AT THE LAB.
LAB?
MY HOUSE.
WE'LL GO OVER EVERYTHING, AND I ASSURE YOU, BY THE END OF THE DAY, WE'LL FIND OUR CULPRIT.

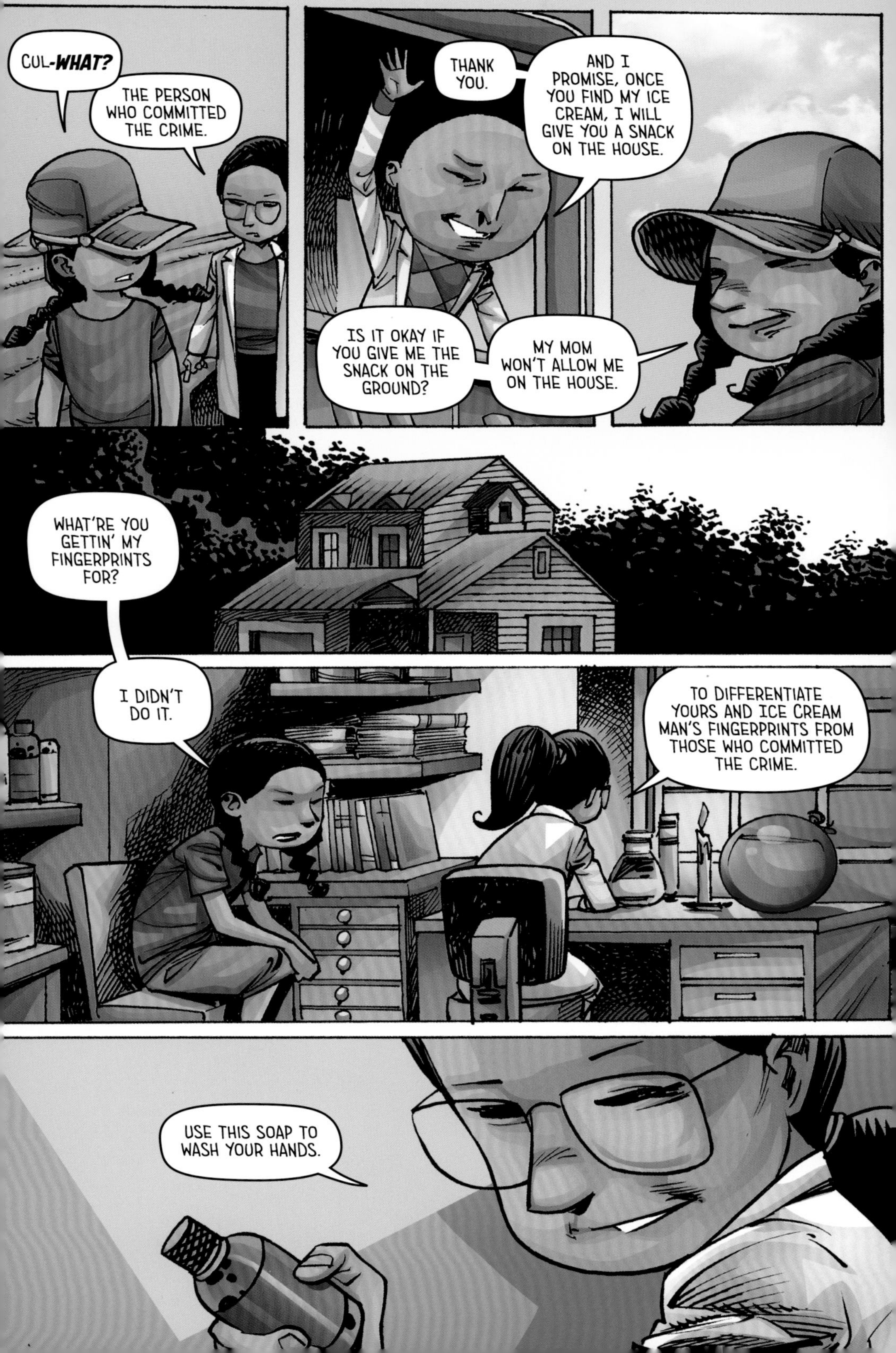
CUL-**WHAT?**
THE PERSON WHO COMMITTED THE CRIME.
THANK YOU.
AND I PROMISE, ONCE YOU FIND MY ICE CREAM, I WILL GIVE YOU A SNACK ON THE HOUSE.
IS IT OKAY IF YOU GIVE ME THE SNACK ON THE GROUND?
MY MOM WON'T ALLOW ME ON THE HOUSE.
WHAT'RE YOU GETTIN' MY FINGERPRINTS FOR?
I DIDN'T DO IT.
TO DIFFERENTIATE YOURS AND ICE CREAM MAN'S FINGERPRINTS FROM THOSE WHO COMMITTED THE CRIME.
USE THIS SOAP TO WASH YOUR HANDS.

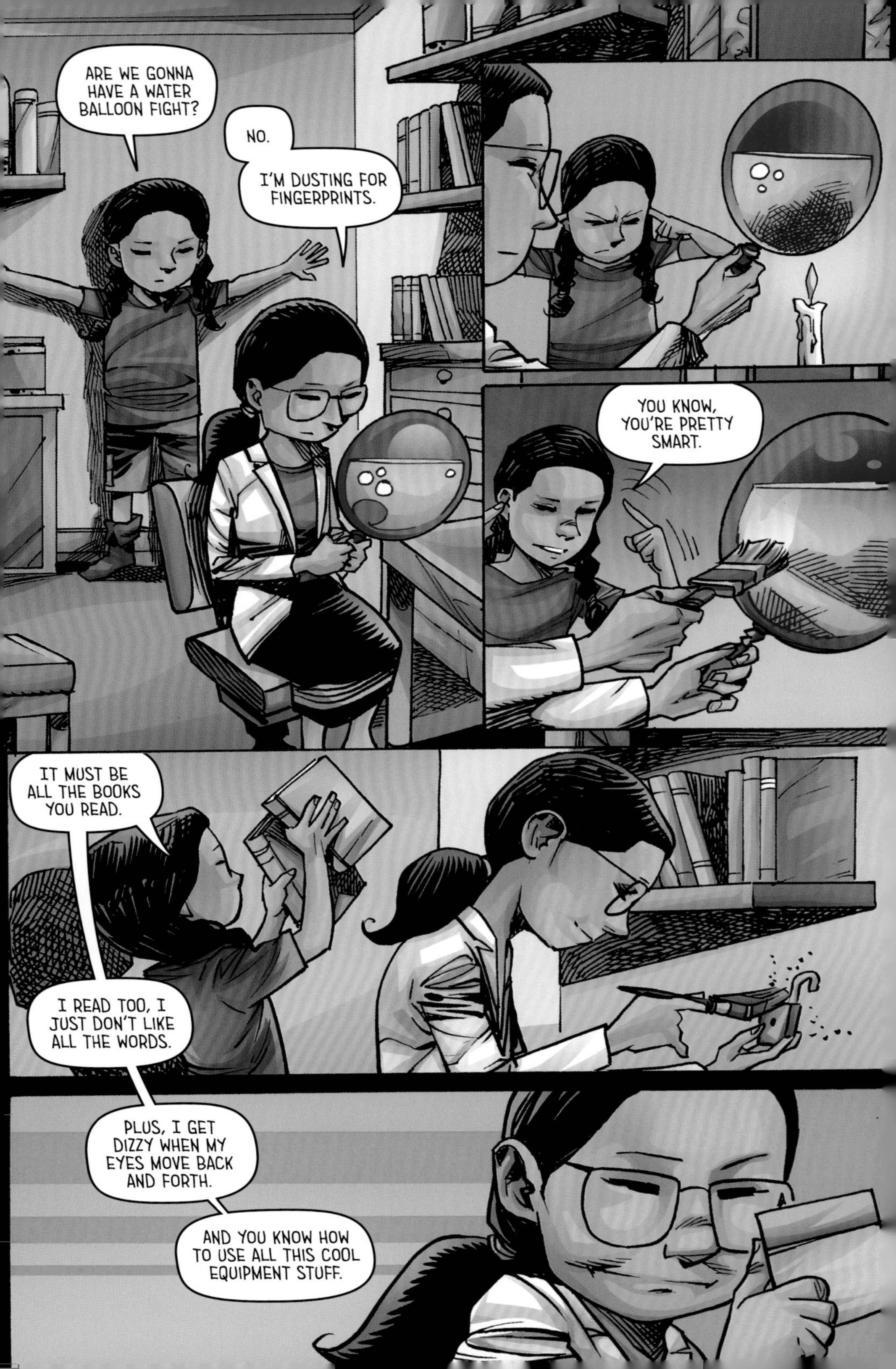
ARE WE GONNA HAVE A WATER BALLOON FIGHT?
NO.
I'M DUSTING FOR FINGERPRINTS.
YOU KNOW, YOU'RE PRETTY SMART.
IT MUST BE ALL THE BOOKS YOU READ.
I READ TOO, I JUST DON'T LIKE ALL THE WORDS.
PLUS, I GET DIZZY WHEN MY EYES MOVE BACK AND FORTH.
AND YOU KNOW HOW TO USE ALL THIS COOL EQUIPMENT STUFF.

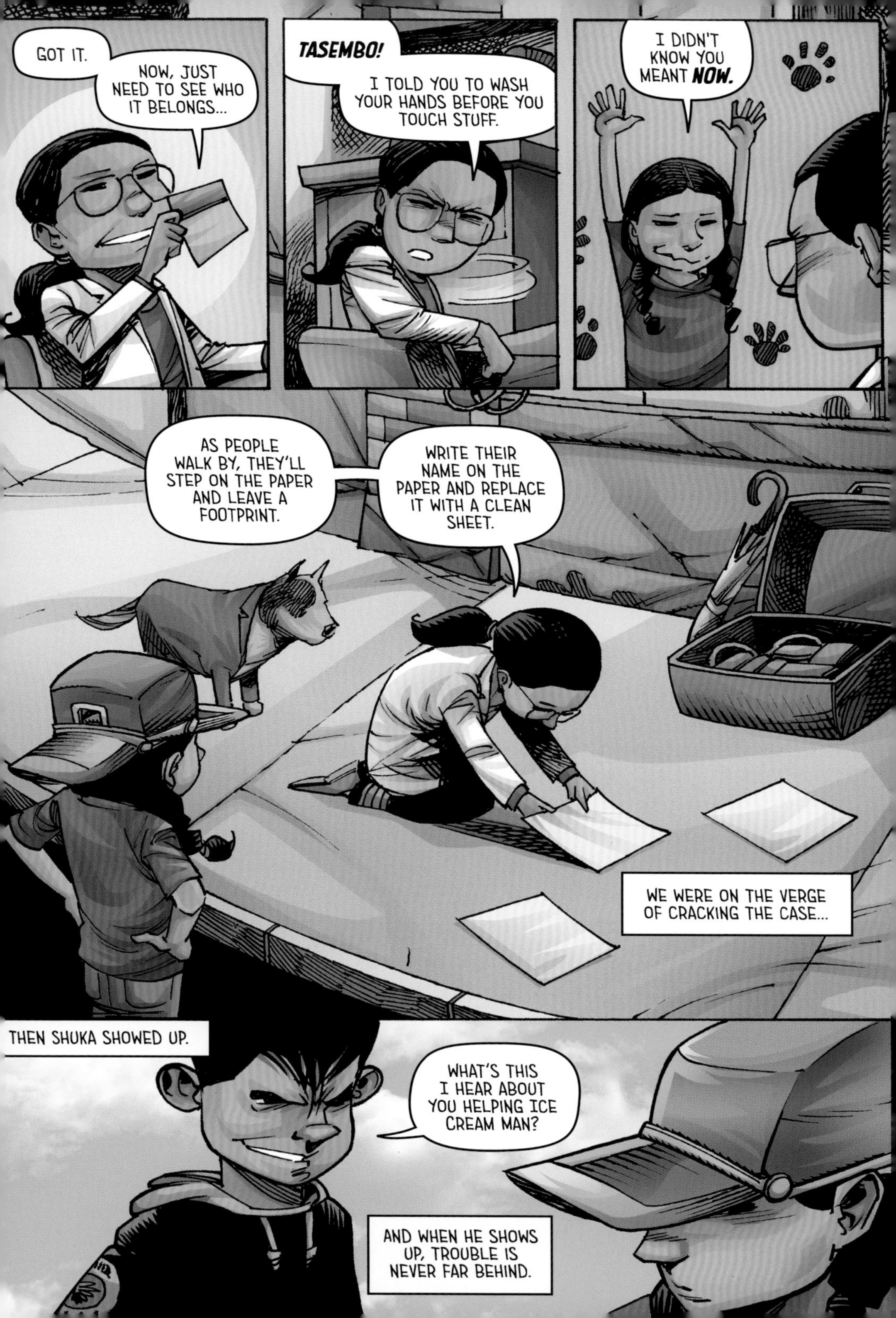
GOT IT.
NOW, JUST NEED TO SEE WHO IT BELONGS...
TASEMBO!
I TOLD YOU TO WASH YOUR HANDS BEFORE YOU TOUCH STUFF.
I DIDN'T KNOW YOU MEANT NOW.
AS PEOPLE WALK BY, THEY'LL STEP ON THE PAPER AND LEAVE A FOOTPRINT.
WRITE THEIR NAME ON THE PAPER AND REPLACE IT WITH A CLEAN SHEET.
WE WERE ON THE VERGE OF CRACKING THE CASE...
THEN SHUKA SHOWED UP.
WHAT'S THIS I HEAR ABOUT YOU HELPING ICE CREAM MAN?
AND WHEN HE SHOWS UP, TROUBLE IS NEVER FAR BEHIND.

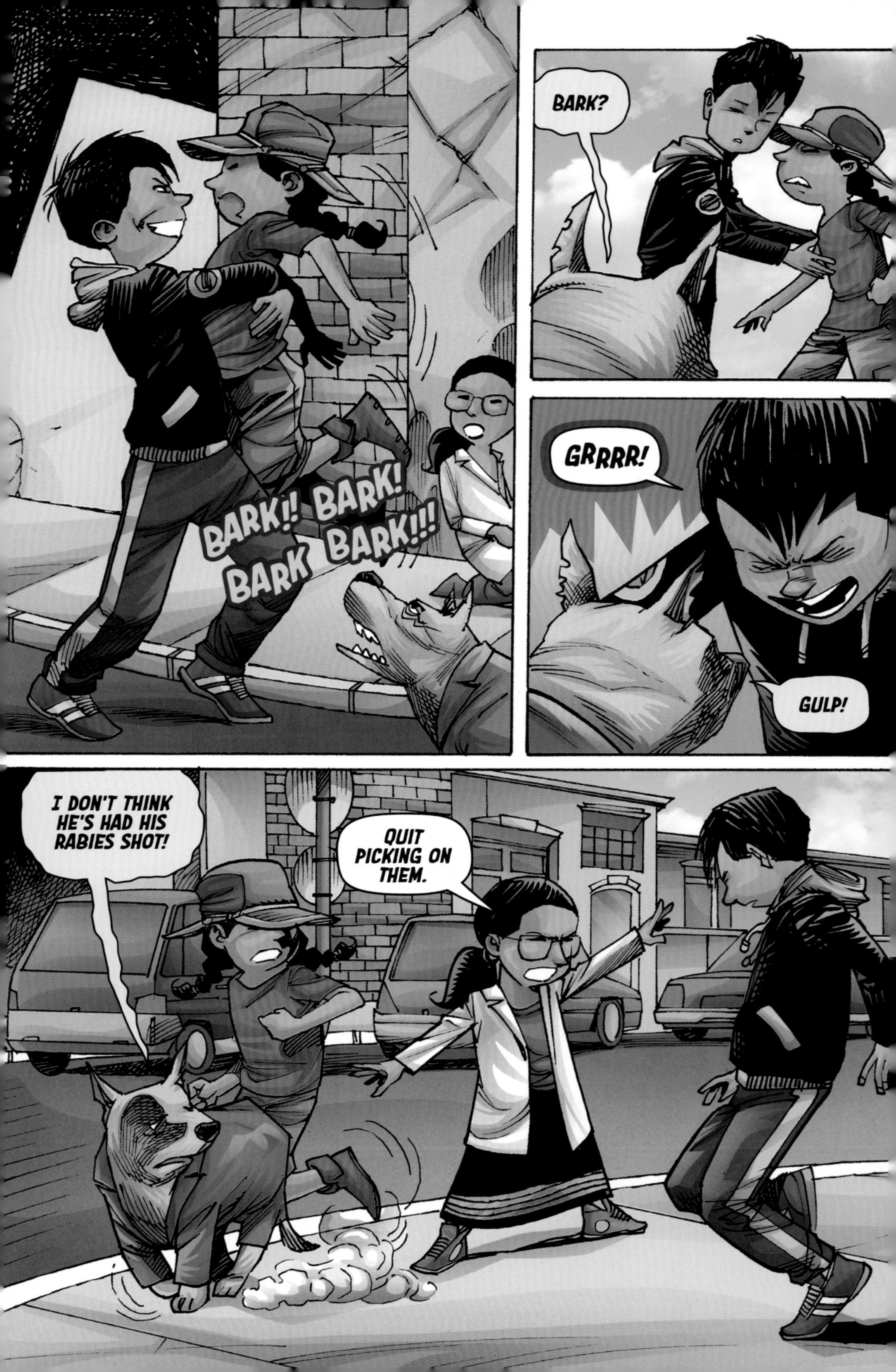
BARK!! BARK!
BARK BARK!!!
BARK?
GRRRR!
GULP!
I DON'T THINK HE'S HAD HIS RABIES SHOT!
QUIT PICKING ON THEM.

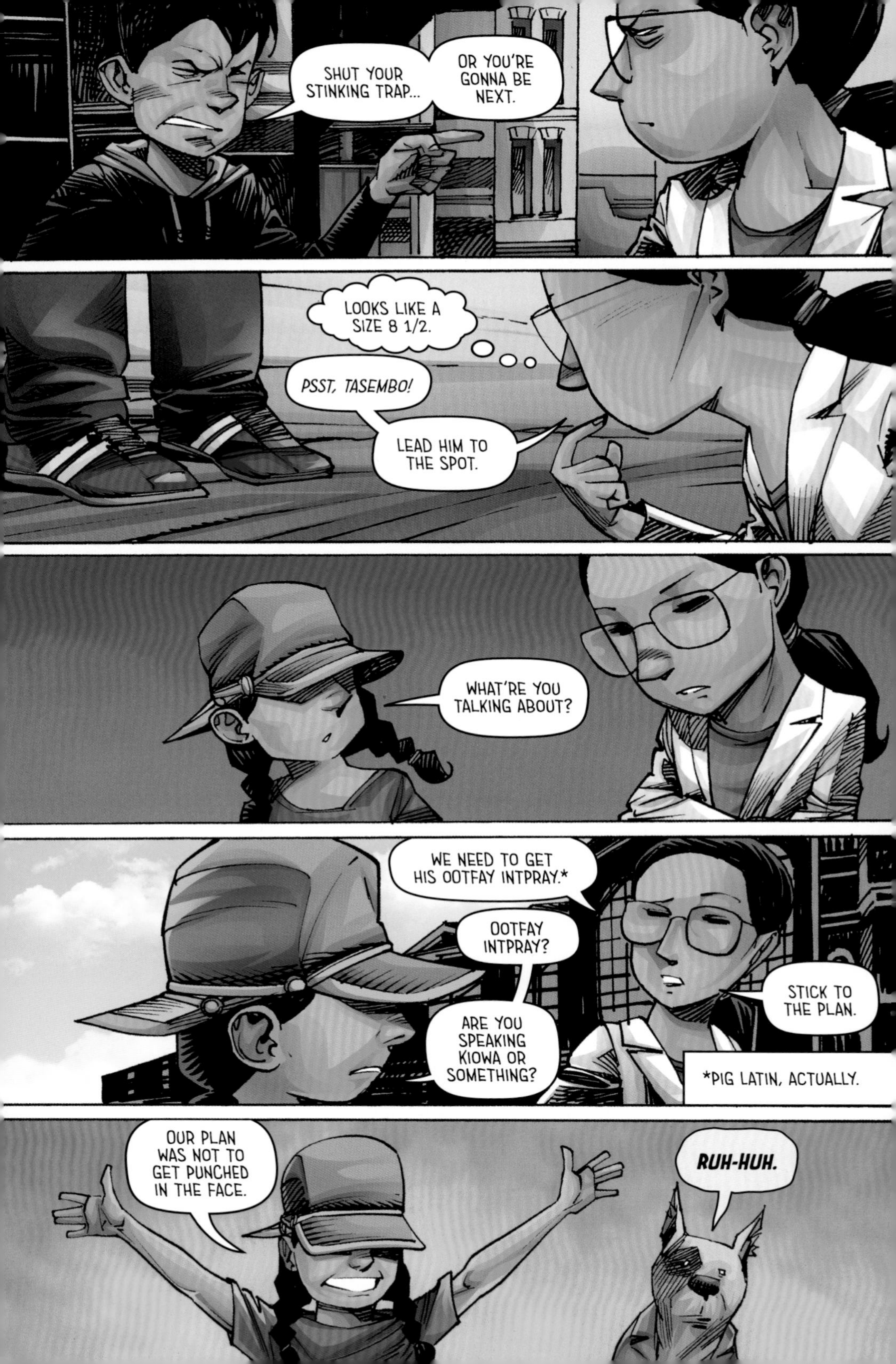
SHUT YOUR STINKING TRAP...
OR YOU'RE GONNA BE NEXT.
LOOKS LIKE A SIZE 8 1/2.
PSST, TASEMBO!
LEAD HIM TO THE SPOT.
WHAT'RE YOU TALKING ABOUT?
WE NEED TO GET HIS OOTFAY INTPRAY.*
OOTFAY INTPRAY?
ARE YOU SPEAKING KIOWA OR SOMETHING?
STICK TO THE PLAN.
*PIG LATIN, ACTUALLY.
OUR PLAN WAS NOT TO GET PUNCHED IN THE FACE.
RUH-HUH.

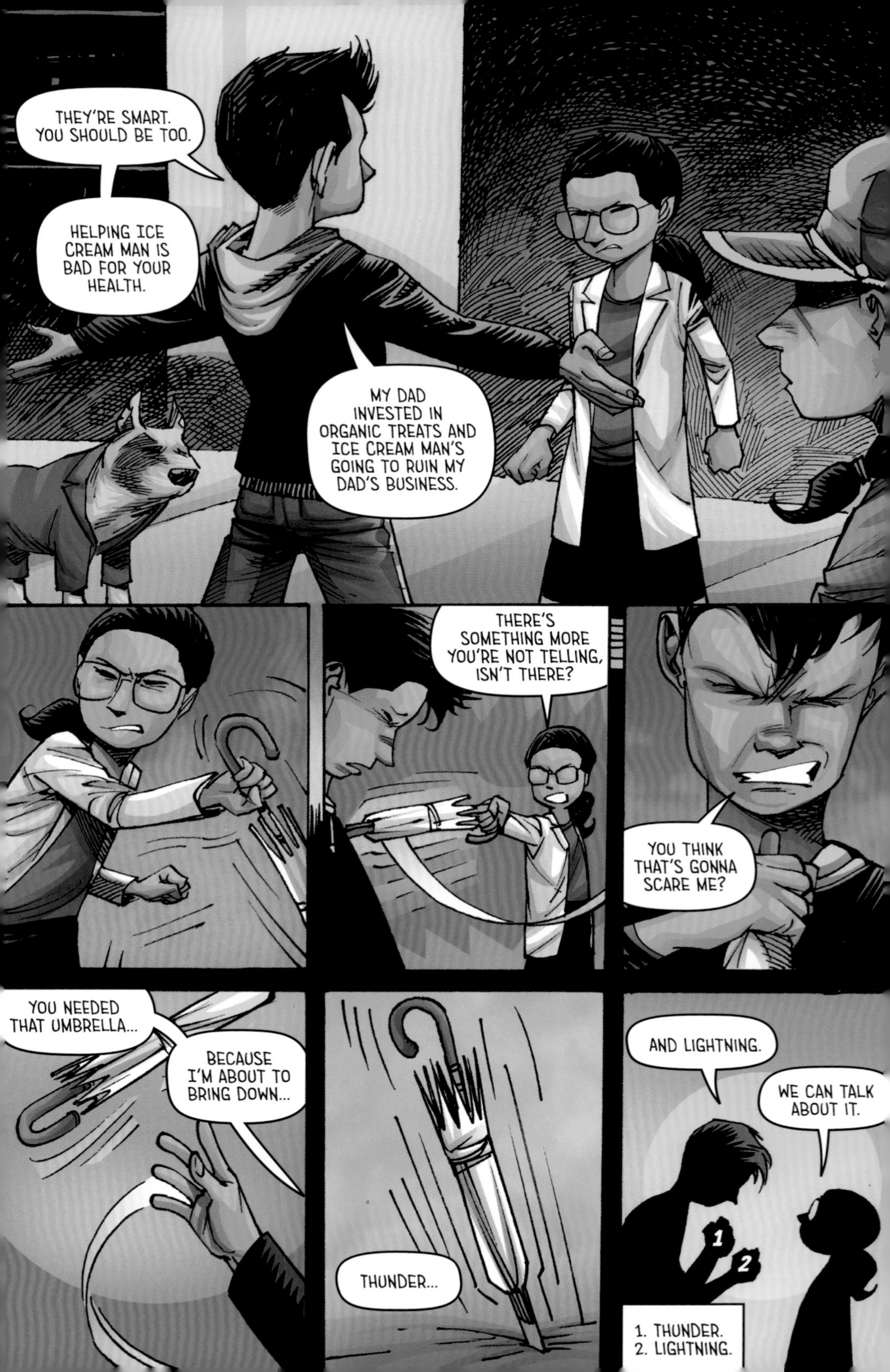
THEY'RE SMART. YOU SHOULD BE TOO.
HELPING ICE CREAM MAN IS BAD FOR YOUR HEALTH.
MY DAD INVESTED IN ORGANIC TREATS AND ICE CREAM MAN'S GOING TO RUIN MY DAD'S BUSINESS.
THERE'S SOMETHING MORE YOU'RE NOT TELLING, ISN'T THERE?
YOU THINK THAT'S GONNA SCARE ME?
YOU NEEDED THAT UMBRELLA...
BECAUSE I'M ABOUT TO BRING DOWN...
THUNDER...
AND LIGHTNING.
WE CAN TALK ABOUT IT.
1
2
1. THUNDER.
2. LIGHTNING.

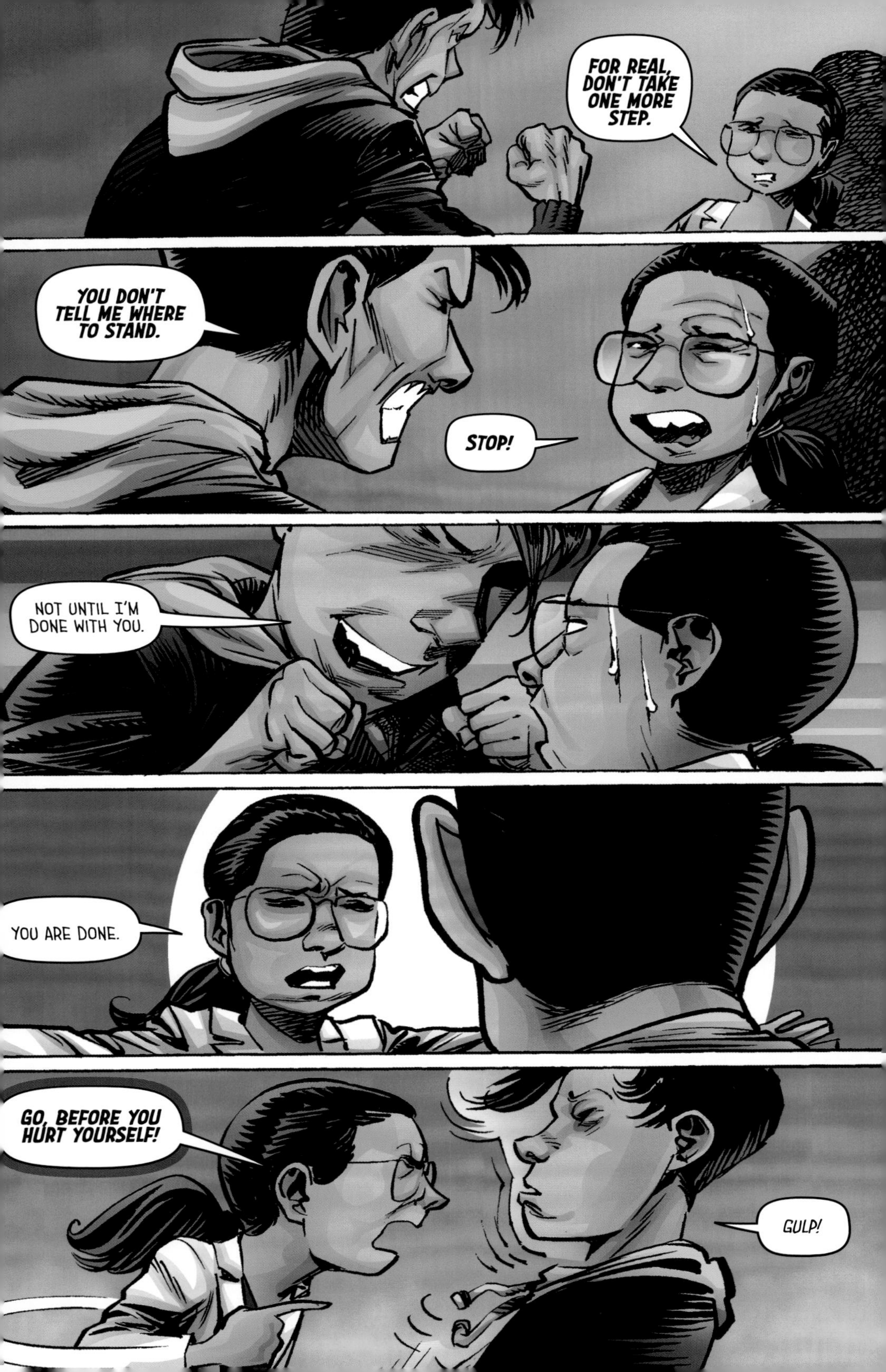
FOR REAL, DON'T TAKE ONE MORE STEP.
YOU DON'T TELL ME WHERE TO STAND.
STOP!
NOT UNTIL I'M DONE WITH YOU.
YOU ARE DONE.
GO, BEFORE YOU HURT YOURSELF!
GULP!

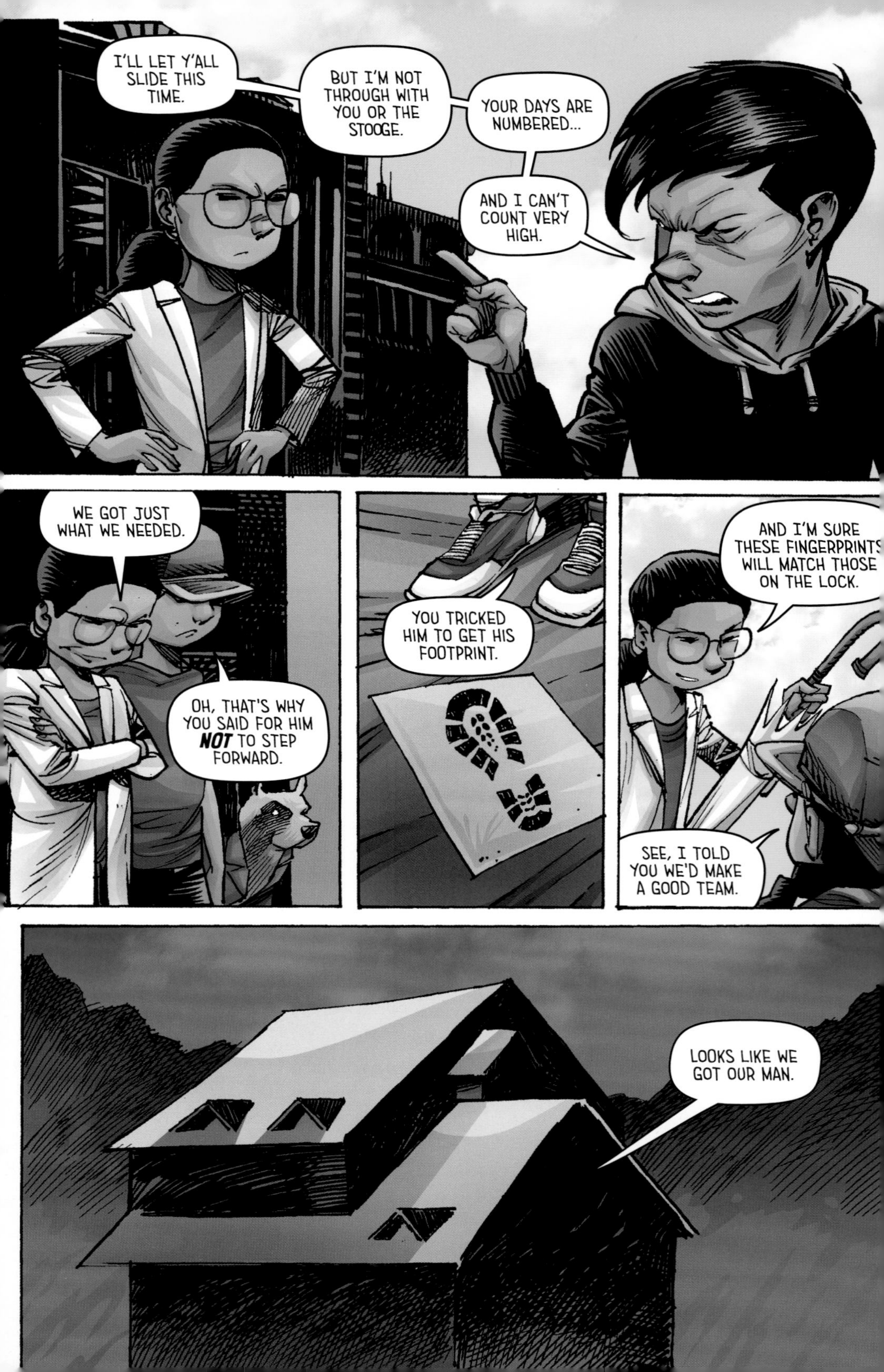
I'LL LET Y'ALL SLIDE THIS TIME.
BUT I'M NOT THROUGH WITH YOU OR THE STOOGE.
YOUR DAYS ARE NUMBERED...
AND I CAN'T COUNT VERY HIGH.
WE GOT JUST WHAT WE NEEDED.
OH, THAT'S WHY YOU SAID FOR HIM **NOT** TO STEP FORWARD.
YOU TRICKED HIM TO GET HIS FOOTPRINT.
AND I'M SURE THESE FINGERPRINTS WILL MATCH THOSE ON THE LOCK.
SEE, I TOLD YOU WE'D MAKE A GOOD TEAM.
LOOKS LIKE WE GOT OUR MAN.

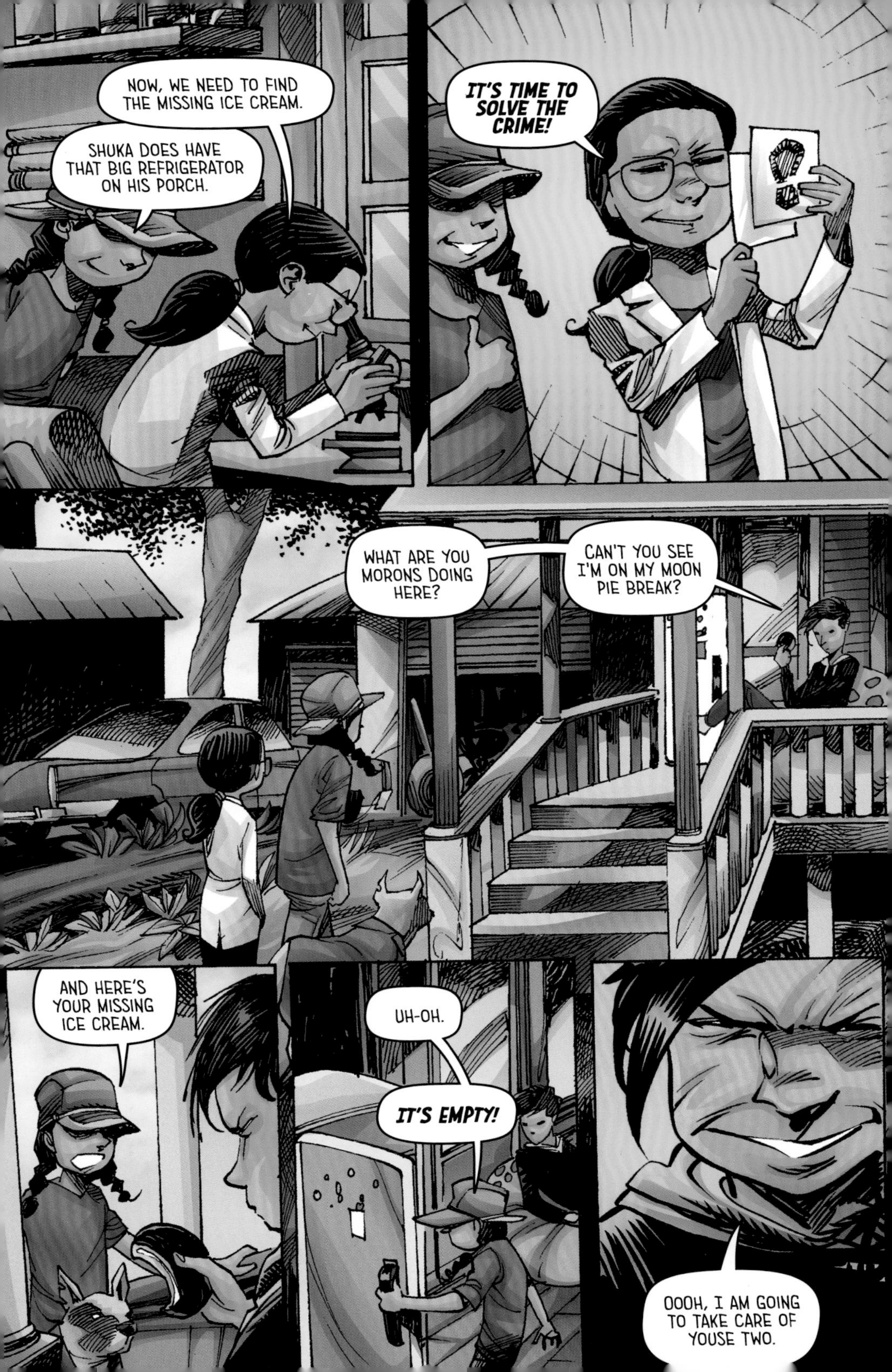
NOW, WE NEED TO FIND THE MISSING ICE CREAM.
SHUKA DOES HAVE THAT BIG REFRIGERATOR ON HIS PORCH.
IT'S TIME TO SOLVE THE CRIME!
WHAT ARE YOU MORONS DOING HERE?
CAN'T YOU SEE I'M ON MY MOON PIE BREAK?
AND HERE'S YOUR MISSING ICE CREAM.
UH-OH.
IT'S EMPTY!
OOOH, I AM GOING TO TAKE CARE OF YOUSE TWO.

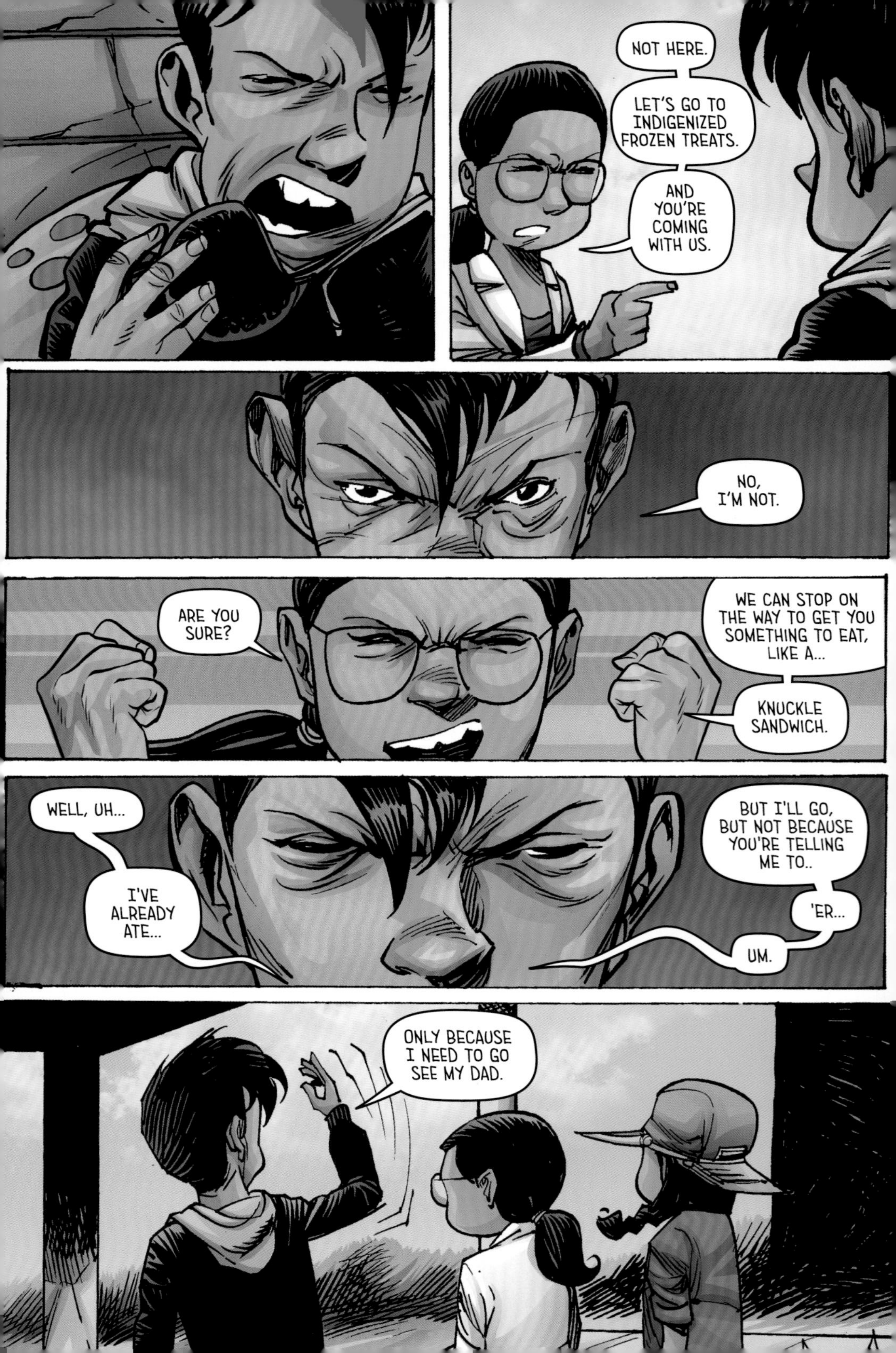
NOT HERE.
LET'S GO TO INDIGENIZED FROZEN TREATS.
AND YOU'RE COMING WITH US.
NO, I'M NOT.
ARE YOU SURE?
WE CAN STOP ON THE WAY TO GET YOU SOMETHING TO EAT, LIKE A...
KNUCKLE SANDWICH.
WELL, UH...
I'VE ALREADY ATE...
BUT I'LL GO, BUT NOT BECAUSE YOU'RE TELLING ME TO..
'ER...
UM.
ONLY BECAUSE I NEED TO GO SEE MY DAD.

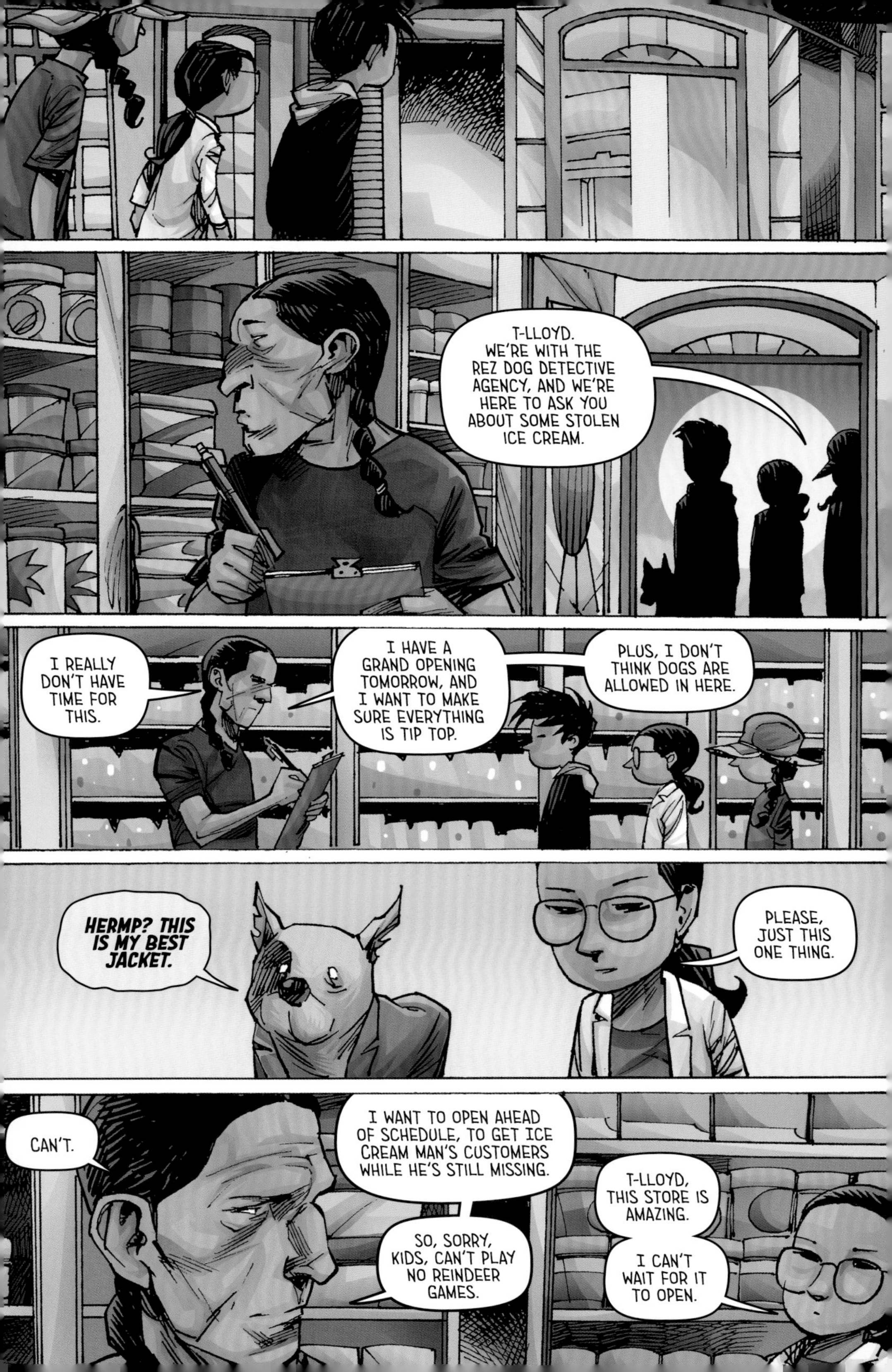
T-LLOYD. WE'RE WITH THE REZ DOG DETECTIVE AGENCY, AND WE'RE HERE TO ASK YOU ABOUT SOME STOLEN ICE CREAM.
I REALLY DON'T HAVE TIME FOR THIS.
I HAVE A GRAND OPENING TOMORROW, AND I WANT TO MAKE SURE EVERYTHING IS TIP TOP.
PLUS, I DON'T THINK DOGS ARE ALLOWED IN HERE.
HERMP? THIS IS MY BEST JACKET.
PLEASE, JUST THIS ONE THING.
CAN'T.
I WANT TO OPEN AHEAD OF SCHEDULE, TO GET ICE CREAM MAN'S CUSTOMERS WHILE HE'S STILL MISSING.
SO, SORRY, KIDS, CAN'T PLAY NO REINDEER GAMES.
T-LLOYD, THIS STORE IS AMAZING.
I CAN'T WAIT FOR IT TO OPEN.

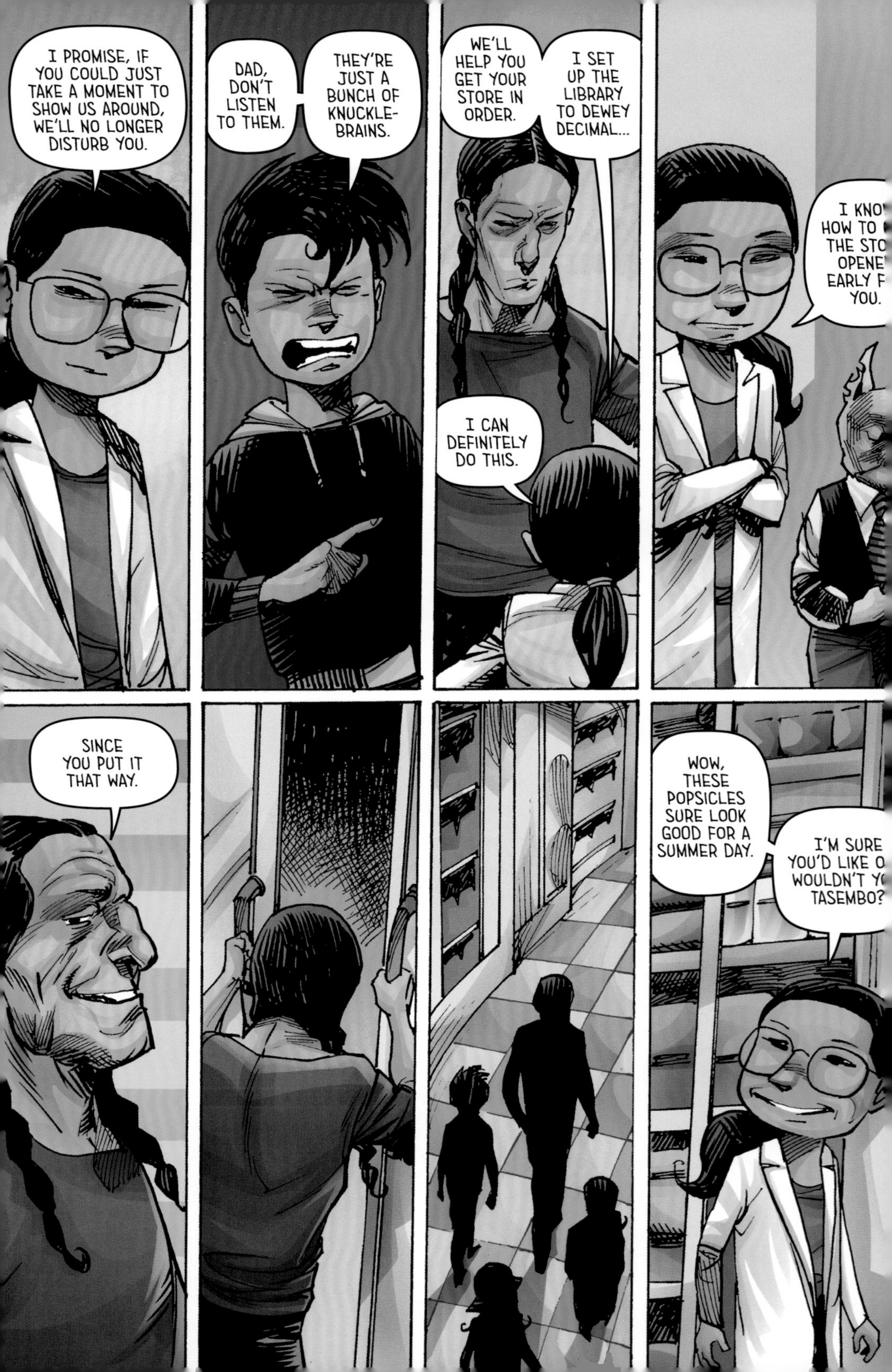
I PROMISE, IF YOU COULD JUST TAKE A MOMENT TO SHOW US AROUND, WE'LL NO LONGER DISTURB YOU.
DAD, DON'T LISTEN TO THEM.
THEY'RE JUST A BUNCH OF KNUCKLE-BRAINS.
WE'LL HELP YOU GET YOUR STORE IN ORDER.
I SET UP THE LIBRARY TO DEWEY DECIMAL...
I CAN DEFINITELY DO THIS.
SINCE YOU PUT IT THAT WAY.
WOW, THESE POPSICLES SURE LOOK GOOD FOR A SUMMER DAY.

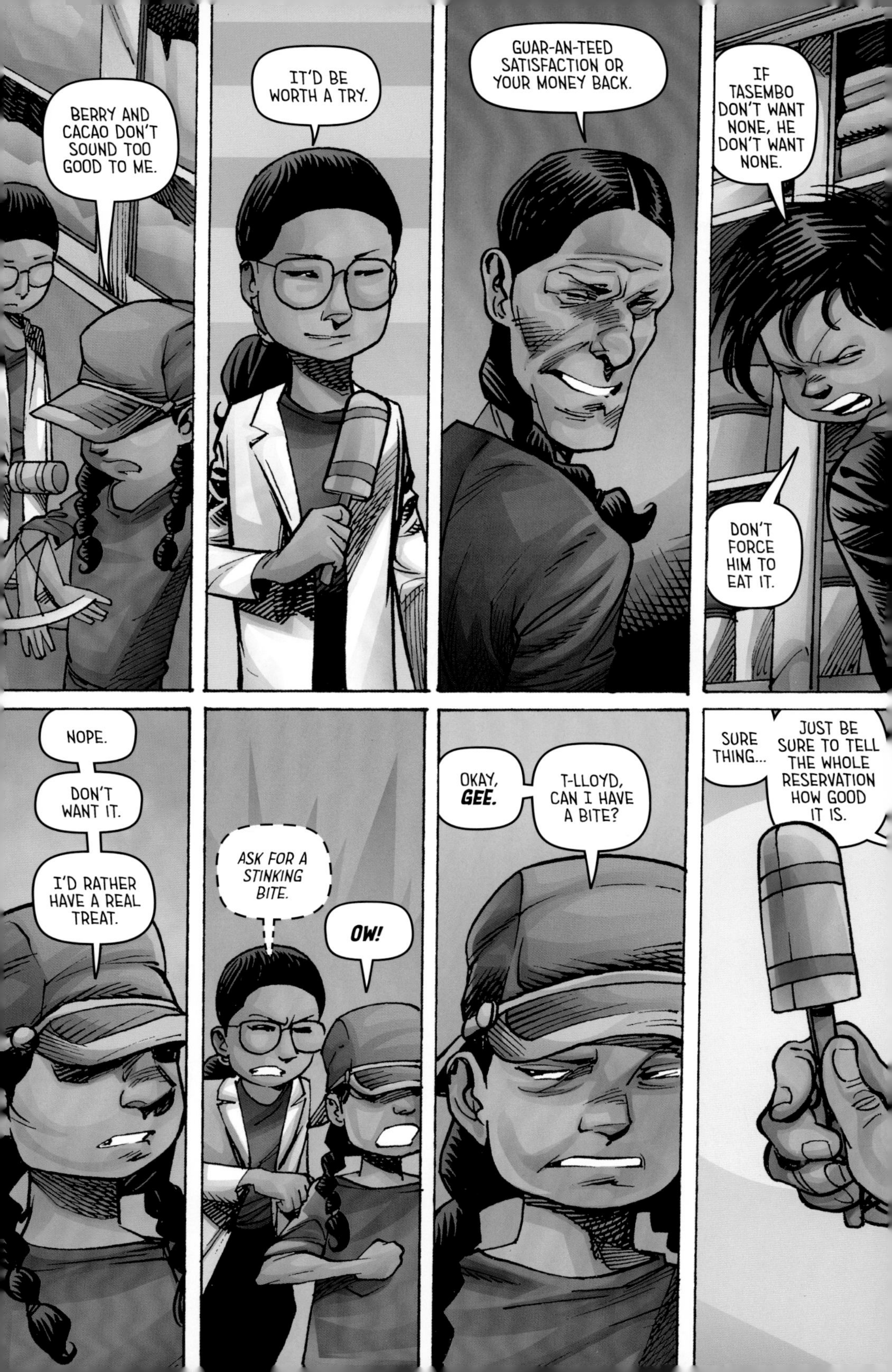
BERRY AND CACAO DON'T SOUND TOO GOOD TO ME.
IT'D BE WORTH A TRY.
GUAR-AN-TEED SATISFACTION OR YOUR MONEY BACK.
IF TASEMBO DON'T WANT NONE, HE DON'T WANT NONE.
DON'T FORCE HIM TO EAT IT.
NOPE.
DON'T WANT IT.
I'D RATHER HAVE A REAL TREAT.
ASK FOR A STINKING BITE.
OW!
OKAY, GEE.
T-LLOYD, CAN I HAVE A BITE?
SURE THING...
JUST BE SURE TO TELL THE WHOLE RESERVATION HOW GOOD IT IS.

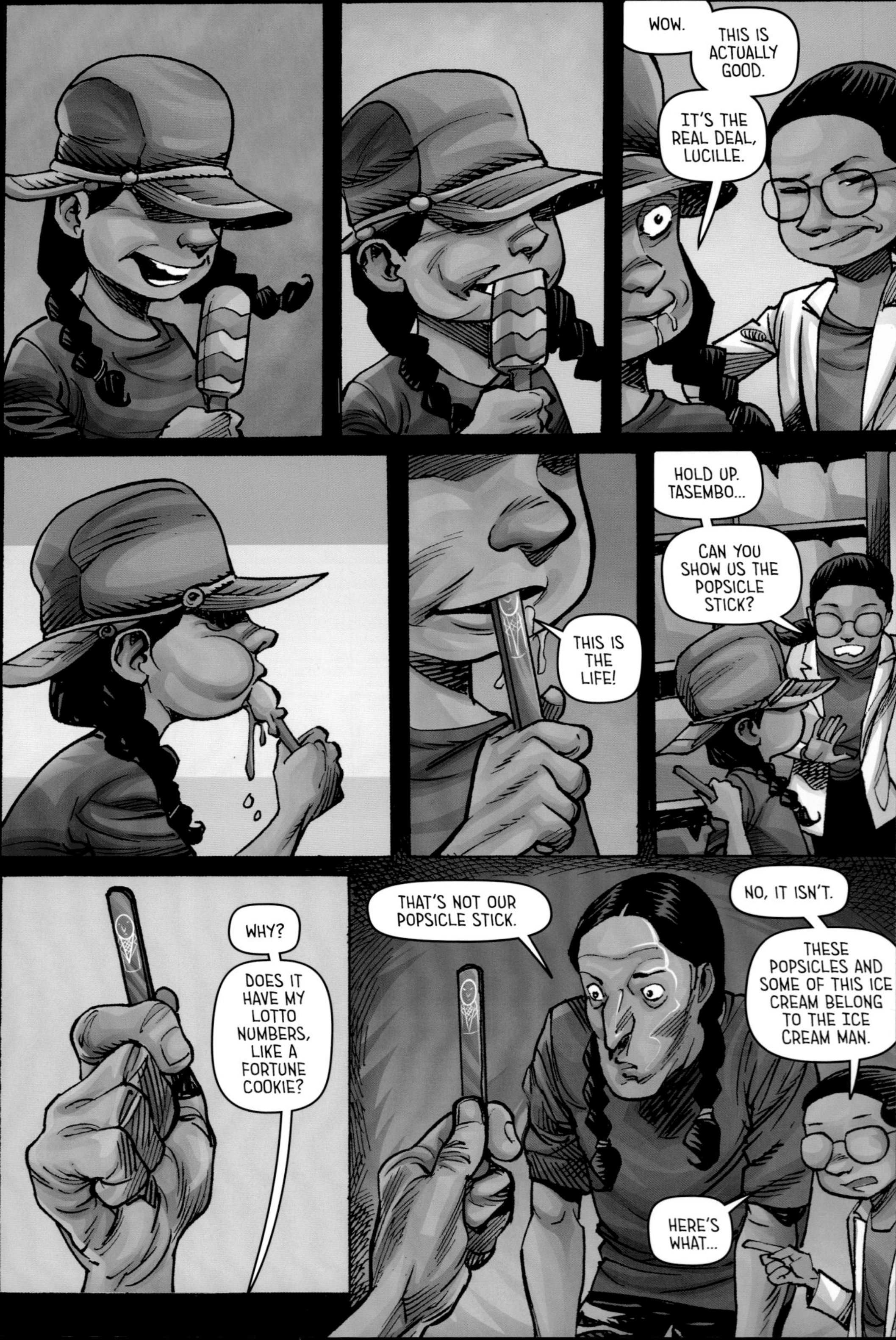
WOW.
THIS IS ACTUALLY GOOD.
IT'S THE REAL DEAL, LUCILLE.
THIS IS THE LIFE!
HOLD UP. TASEMBO...
CAN YOU SHOW US THE POPSICLE STICK?
WHY?
DOES IT HAVE MY LOTTO NUMBERS, LIKE A FORTUNE COOKIE?
THAT'S NOT OUR POPSICLE STICK.
NO, IT ISN'T.
THESE POPSICLES AND SOME OF THIS ICE CREAM BELONG TO THE ICE CREAM MAN.
HERE'S WHAT...

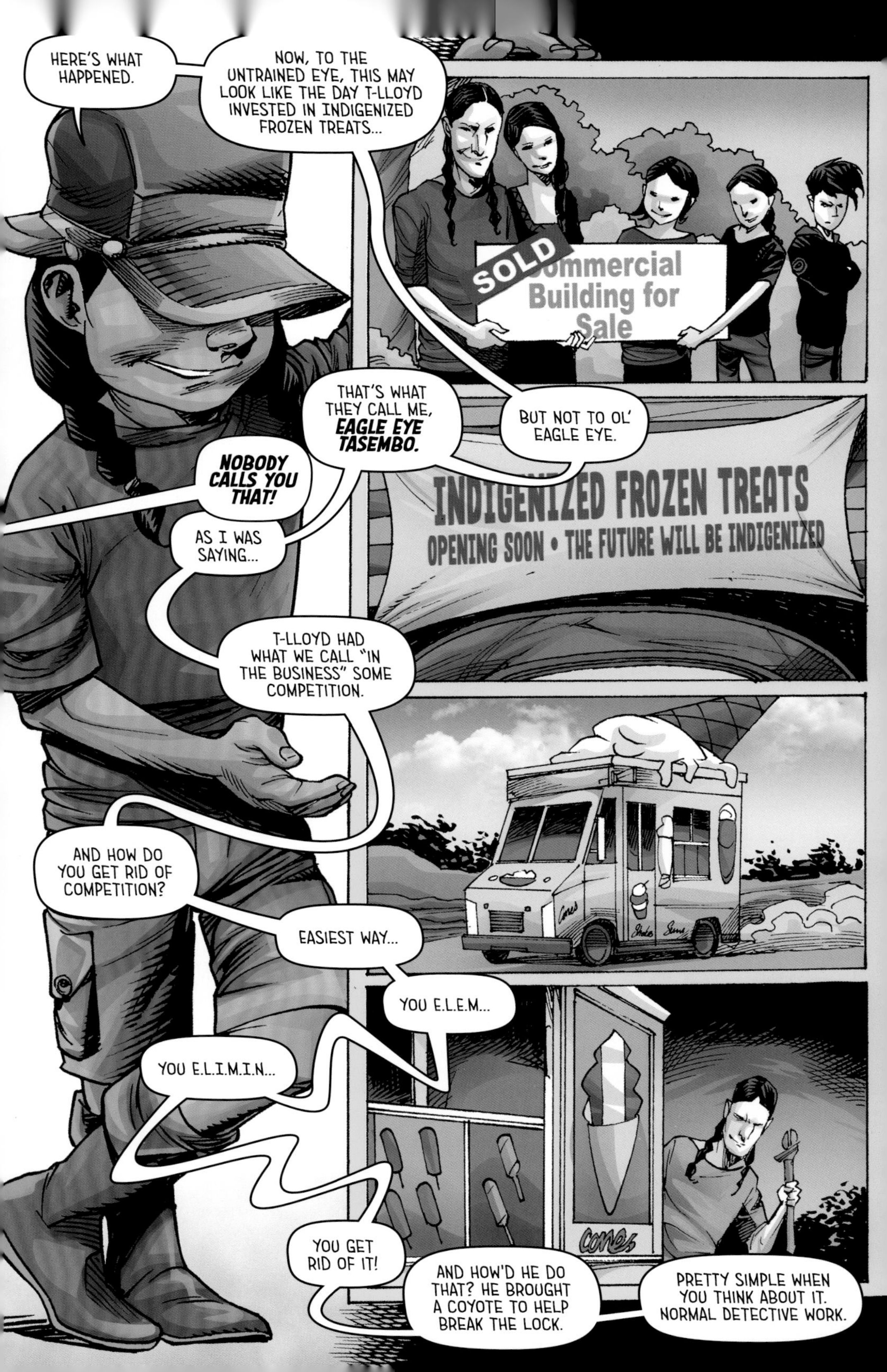
HERE'S WHAT HAPPENED.
NOW, TO THE UNTRAINED EYE, THIS MAY LOOK LIKE THE DAY T-LLOYD INVESTED IN INDIGENIZED FROZEN TREATS...
SOLD
Commercial Building for Sale
BUT NOT TO OL' EAGLE EYE.
THAT'S WHAT THEY CALL ME, EAGLE EYE TASEMBO.
NOBODY CALLS YOU THAT!
AS I WAS SAYING...
INDIGENIZED FROZEN TREATS
OPENING SOON • THE FUTURE WILL BE INDIGENIZED
T-LLOYD HAD WHAT WE CALL "IN THE BUSINESS" SOME COMPETITION.
AND HOW DO YOU GET RID OF COMPETITION?
EASIEST WAY...
YOU E.L.E.M...
YOU E.L.I.M.I.N...
YOU GET RID OF IT!
Cones
AND HOW'D HE DO THAT? HE BROUGHT A COYOTE TO HELP BREAK THE LOCK.
PRETTY SIMPLE WHEN YOU THINK ABOUT IT. NORMAL DETECTIVE WORK.

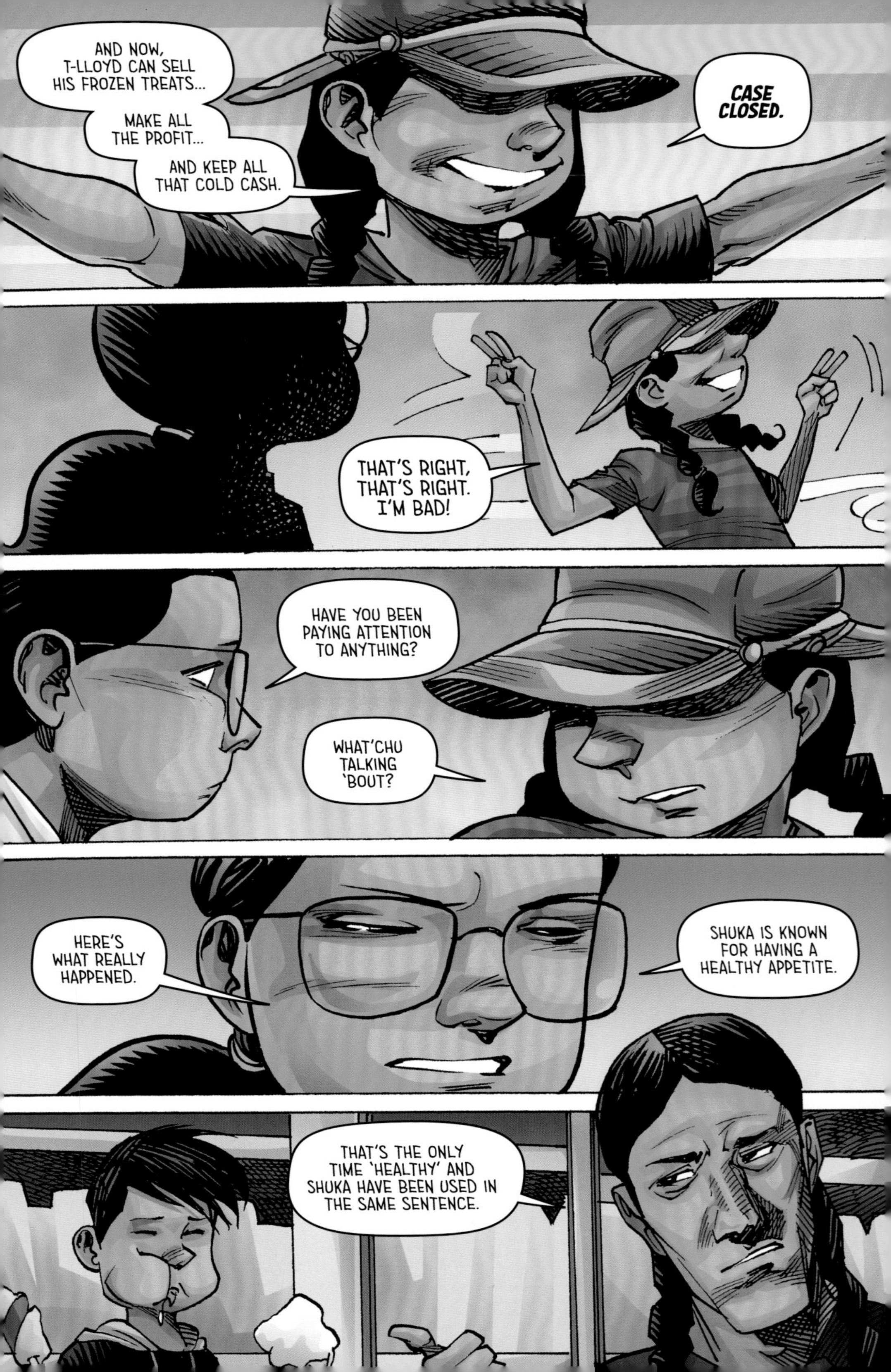
AND NOW, T-LLOYD CAN SELL HIS FROZEN TREATS...
MAKE ALL THE PROFIT...
AND KEEP ALL THAT COLD CASH.
CASE CLOSED.
THAT'S RIGHT, THAT'S RIGHT. I'M BAD!
HAVE YOU BEEN PAYING ATTENTION TO ANYTHING?
WHAT'CHU TALKING 'BOUT?
HERE'S WHAT REALLY HAPPENED.
SHUKA IS KNOWN FOR HAVING A HEALTHY APPETITE.
THAT'S THE ONLY TIME 'HEALTHY' AND SHUKA HAVE BEEN USED IN THE SAME SENTENCE.

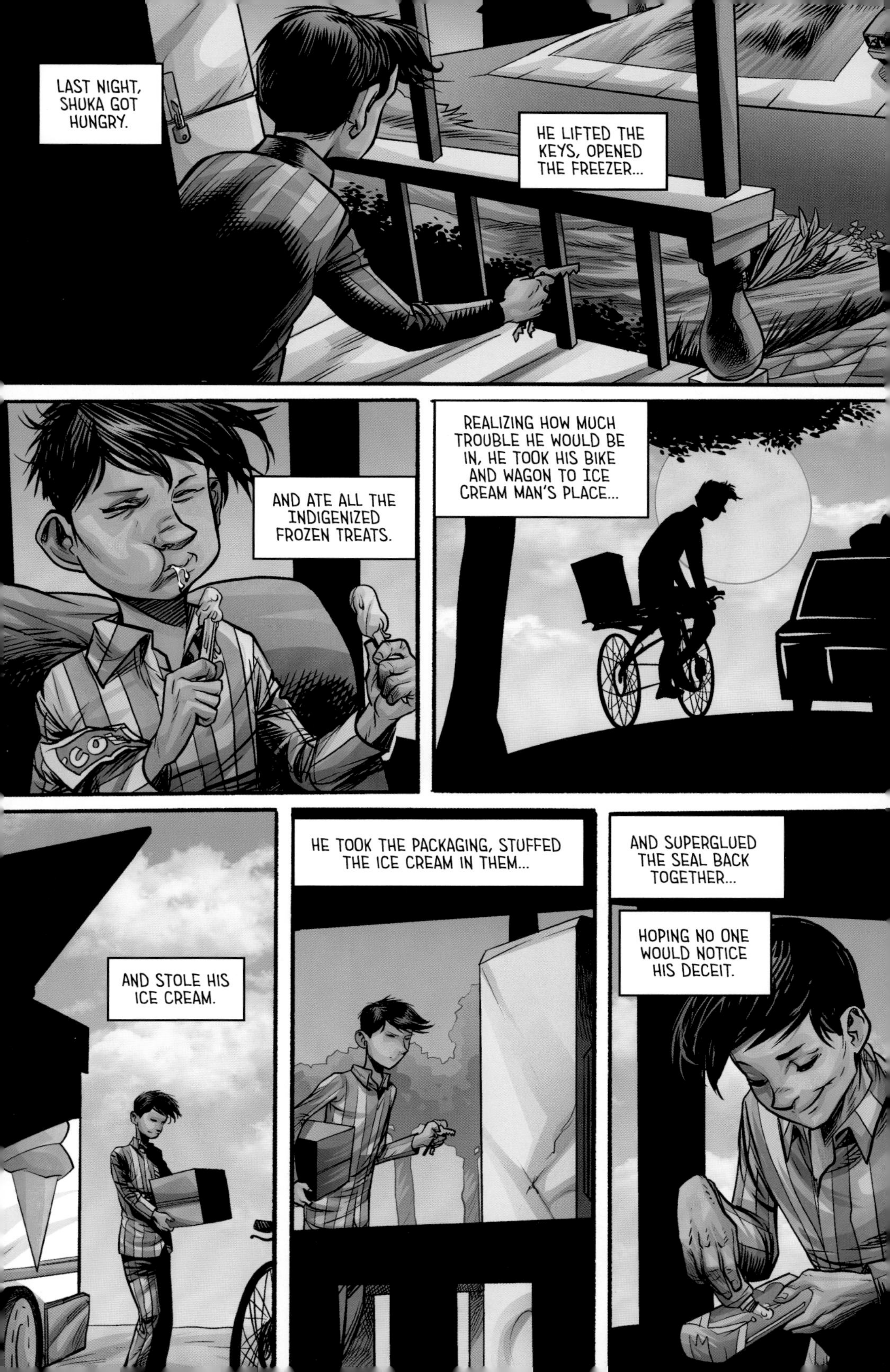
LAST NIGHT, SHUKA GOT HUNGRY.
HE LIFTED THE KEYS, OPENED THE FREEZER...
AND ATE ALL THE INDIGENIZED FROZEN TREATS.
REALIZING HOW MUCH TROUBLE HE WOULD BE IN, HE TOOK HIS BIKE AND WAGON TO ICE CREAM MAN'S PLACE...
AND STOLE HIS ICE CREAM.
HE TOOK THE PACKAGING, STUFFED THE ICE CREAM IN THEM...
AND SUPERGLUED THE SEAL BACK TOGETHER...
HOPING NO ONE WOULD NOTICE HIS DECEIT.

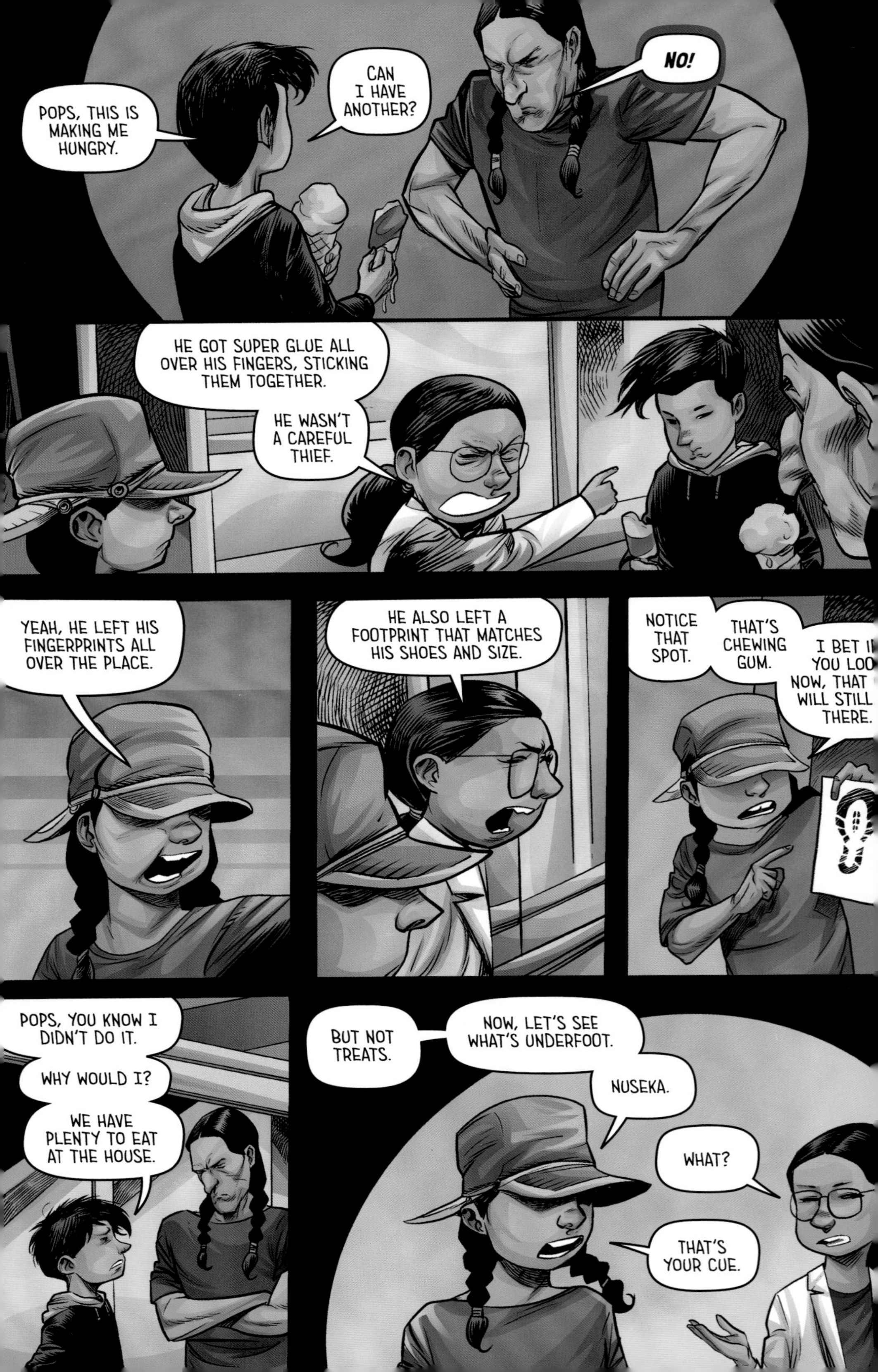
POPS, THIS IS MAKING ME HUNGRY.
CAN I HAVE ANOTHER?
NO!
HE GOT SUPER GLUE ALL OVER HIS FINGERS, STICKING THEM TOGETHER.
HE WASN'T A CAREFUL THIEF.
YEAH, HE LEFT HIS FINGERPRINTS ALL OVER THE PLACE.
HE ALSO LEFT A FOOTPRINT THAT MATCHES HIS SHOES AND SIZE.
NOTICE THAT SPOT.
THAT'S CHEWING GUM.
POPS, YOU KNOW I DIDN'T DO IT.
WHY WOULD I?
WE HAVE PLENTY TO EAT AT THE HOUSE.
BUT NOT TREATS.
NOW, LET'S SEE WHAT'S UNDERFOOT.
NUSEKA.
WHAT?
THAT'S YOUR CUE.

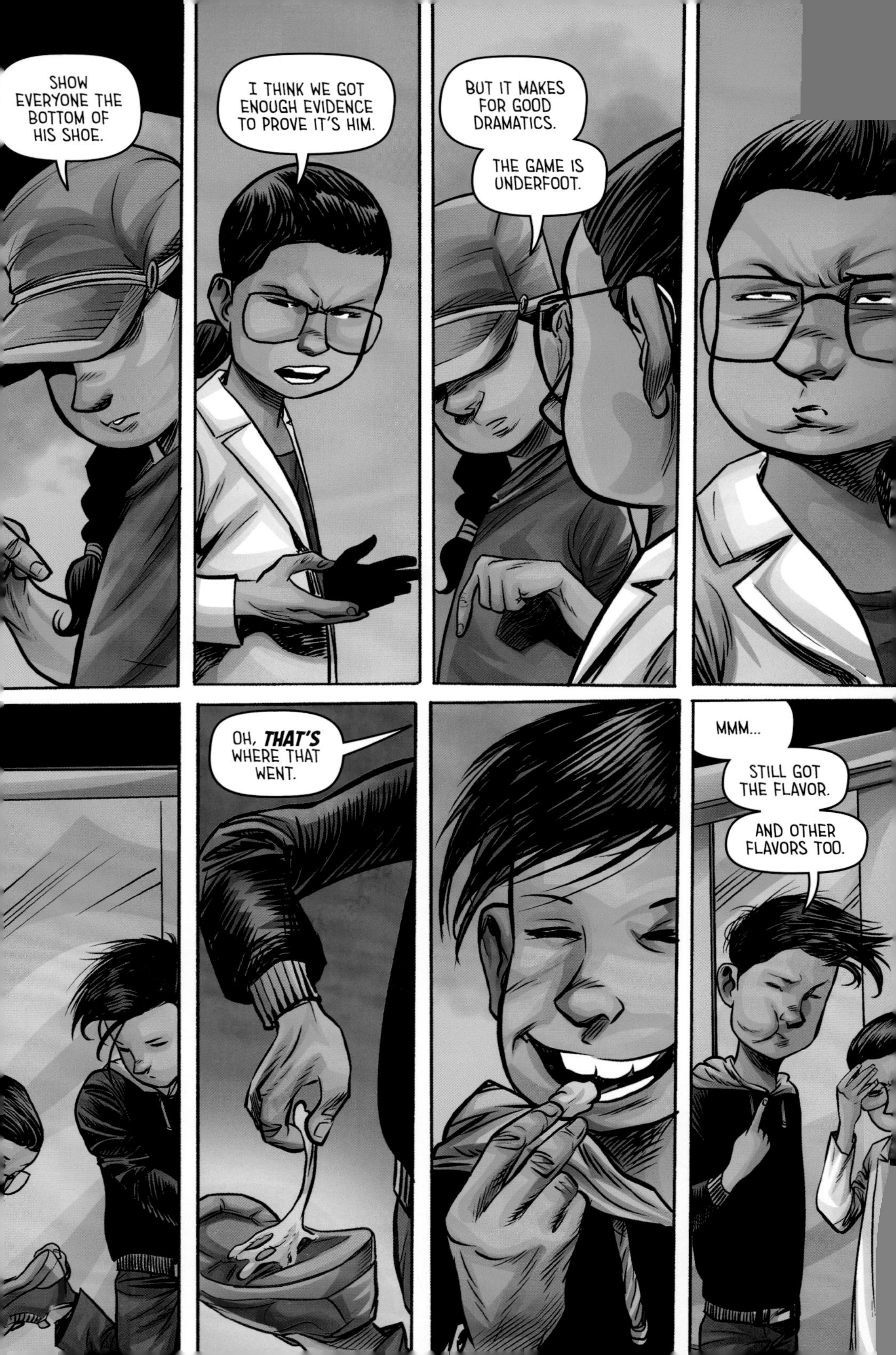
SHOW EVERYONE THE BOTTOM OF HIS SHOE.
I THINK WE GOT ENOUGH EVIDENCE TO PROVE IT'S HIM.
BUT IT MAKES FOR GOOD DRAMATICS.
THE GAME IS UNDERFOOT.
OH, **THAT'S** WHERE THAT WENT.
MMM...
STILL GOT THE FLAVOR.
AND OTHER FLAVORS TOO.

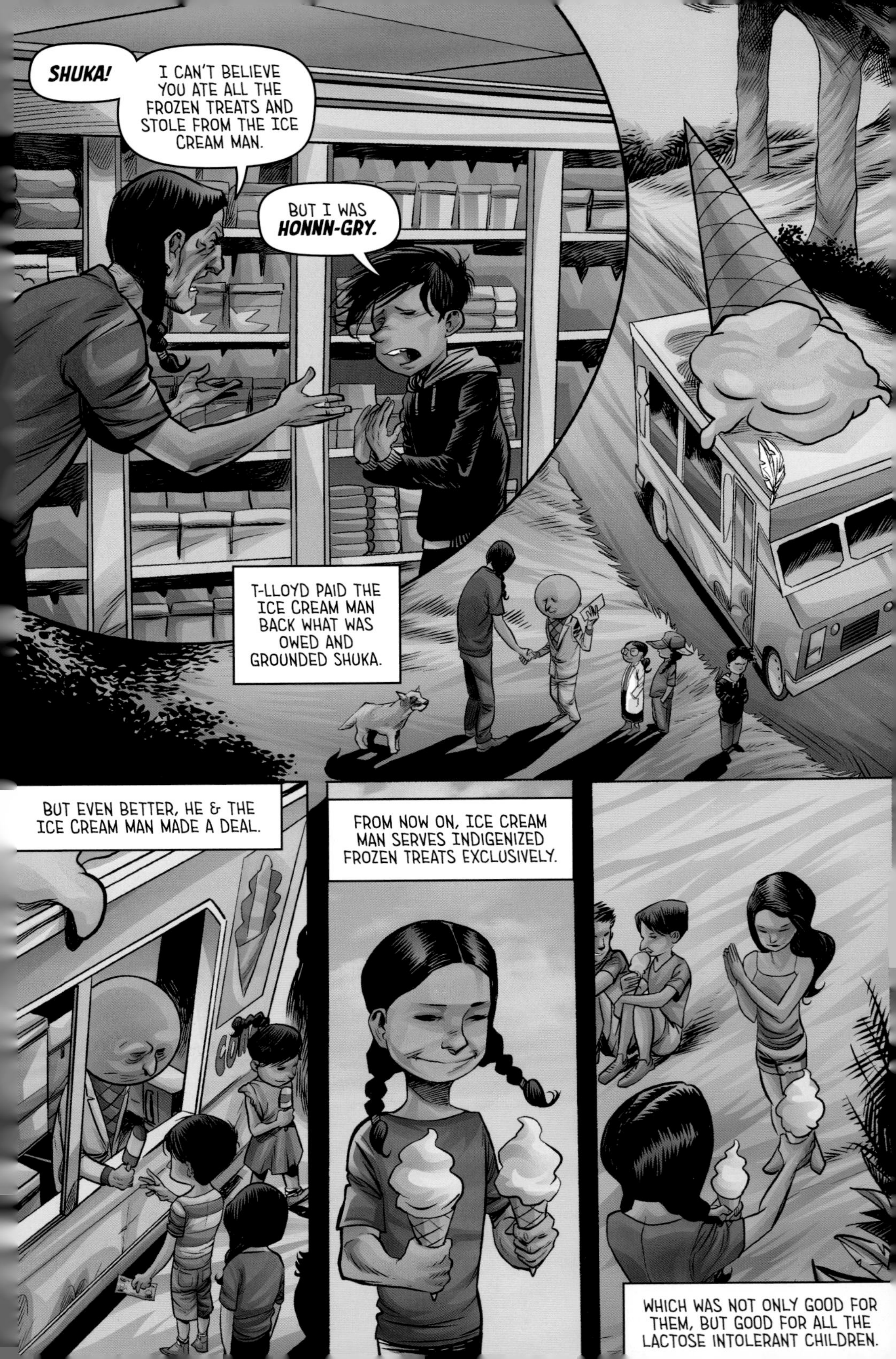
SHUKA!
I CAN'T BELIEVE YOU ATE ALL THE FROZEN TREATS AND STOLE FROM THE ICE CREAM MAN.
BUT I WAS HONNN-GRY.
T-LLOYD PAID THE ICE CREAM MAN BACK WHAT WAS OWED AND GROUNDED SHUKA.
BUT EVEN BETTER, HE & THE ICE CREAM MAN MADE A DEAL.
FROM NOW ON, ICE CREAM MAN SERVES INDIGENIZED FROZEN TREATS EXCLUSIVELY.
WHICH WAS NOT ONLY GOOD FOR THEM, BUT GOOD FOR ALL THE LACTOSE INTOLERANT CHILDREN.

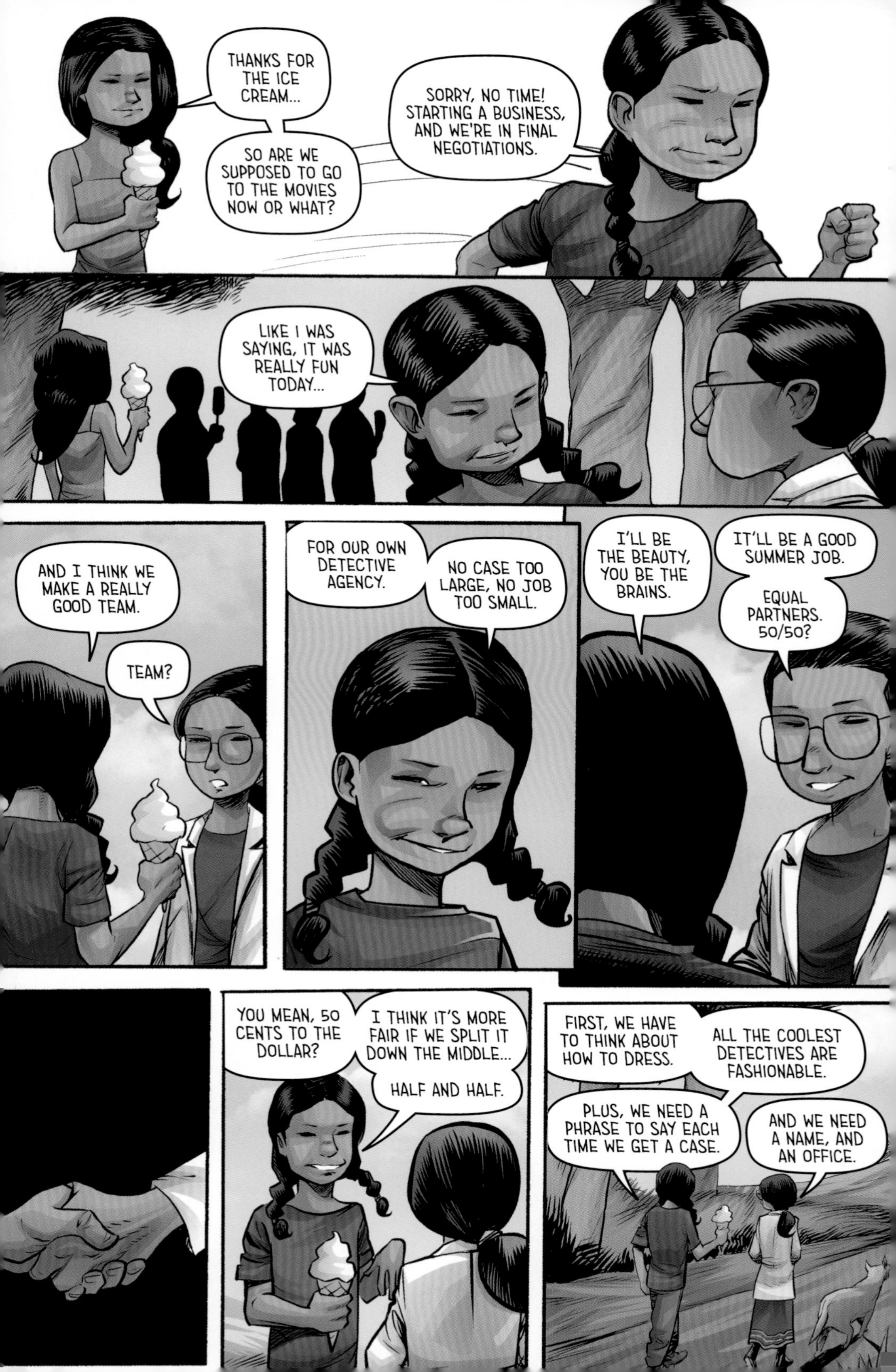
THANKS FOR THE ICE CREAM...
SO ARE WE SUPPOSED TO GO TO THE MOVIES NOW OR WHAT?
SORRY, NO TIME! STARTING A BUSINESS, AND WE'RE IN FINAL NEGOTIATIONS.
LIKE I WAS SAYING, IT WAS REALLY FUN TODAY...
AND I THINK WE MAKE A REALLY GOOD TEAM.
TEAM?
FOR OUR OWN DETECTIVE AGENCY.
NO CASE TOO LARGE, NO JOB TOO SMALL.
I'LL BE THE BEAUTY, YOU BE THE BRAINS.
IT'LL BE A GOOD SUMMER JOB.
EQUAL PARTNERS. 50/50?
YOU MEAN, 50 CENTS TO THE DOLLAR?
I THINK IT'S MORE FAIR IF WE SPLIT IT DOWN THE MIDDLE...
HALF AND HALF.
FIRST, WE HAVE TO THINK ABOUT HOW TO DRESS.
ALL THE COOLEST DETECTIVES ARE FASHIONABLE.
PLUS, WE NEED A PHRASE TO SAY EACH TIME WE GET A CASE.
AND WE NEED A NAME, AND AN OFFICE.

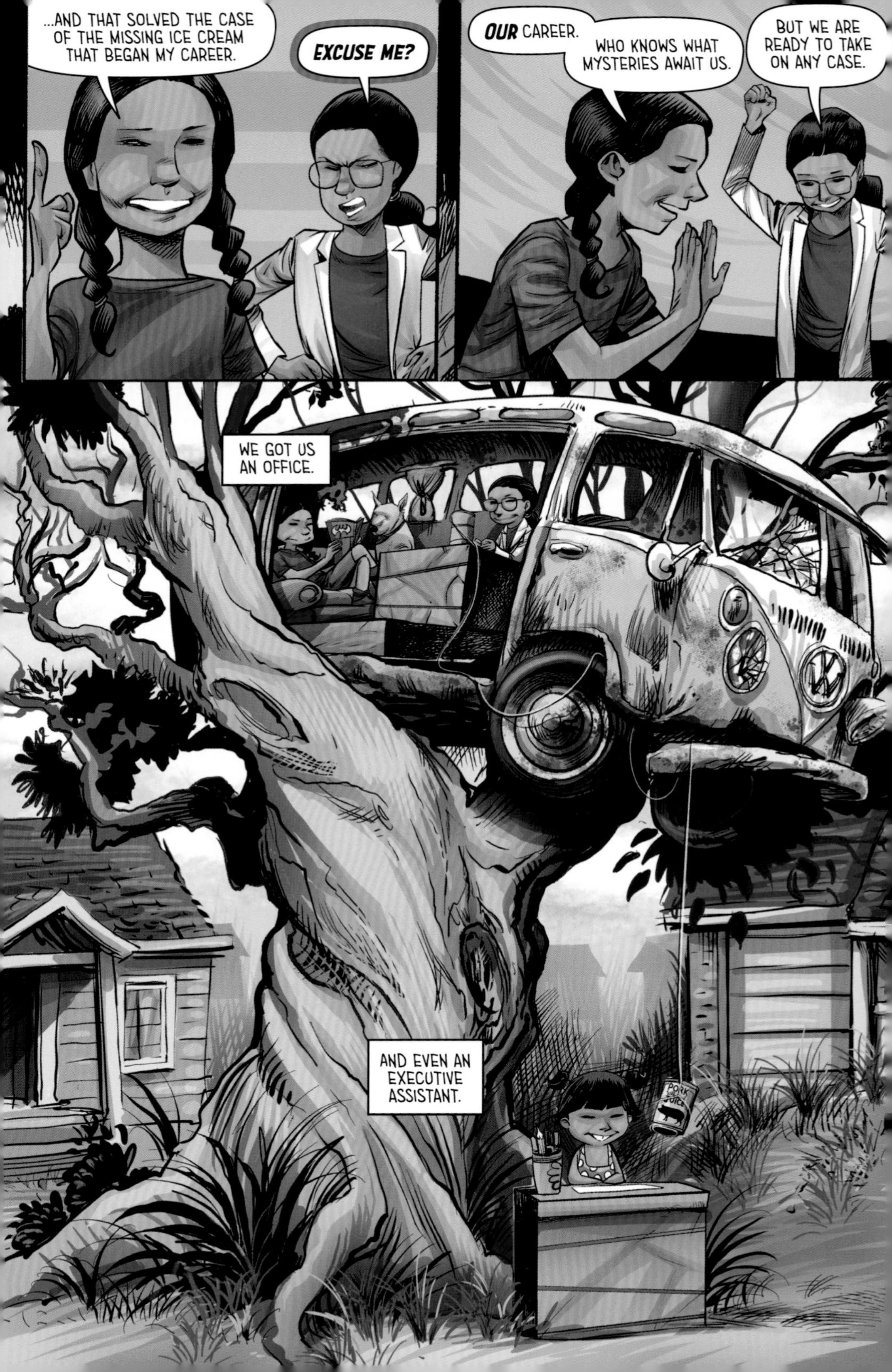
...AND THAT SOLVED THE CASE OF THE MISSING ICE CREAM THAT BEGAN MY CAREER.
EXCUSE ME?
OUR CAREER.
WHO KNOWS WHAT MYSTERIES AWAIT US.
BUT WE ARE READY TO TAKE ON ANY CASE.
WE GOT US AN OFFICE.
AND EVEN AN EXECUTIVE ASSISTANT.
PORK JUICE

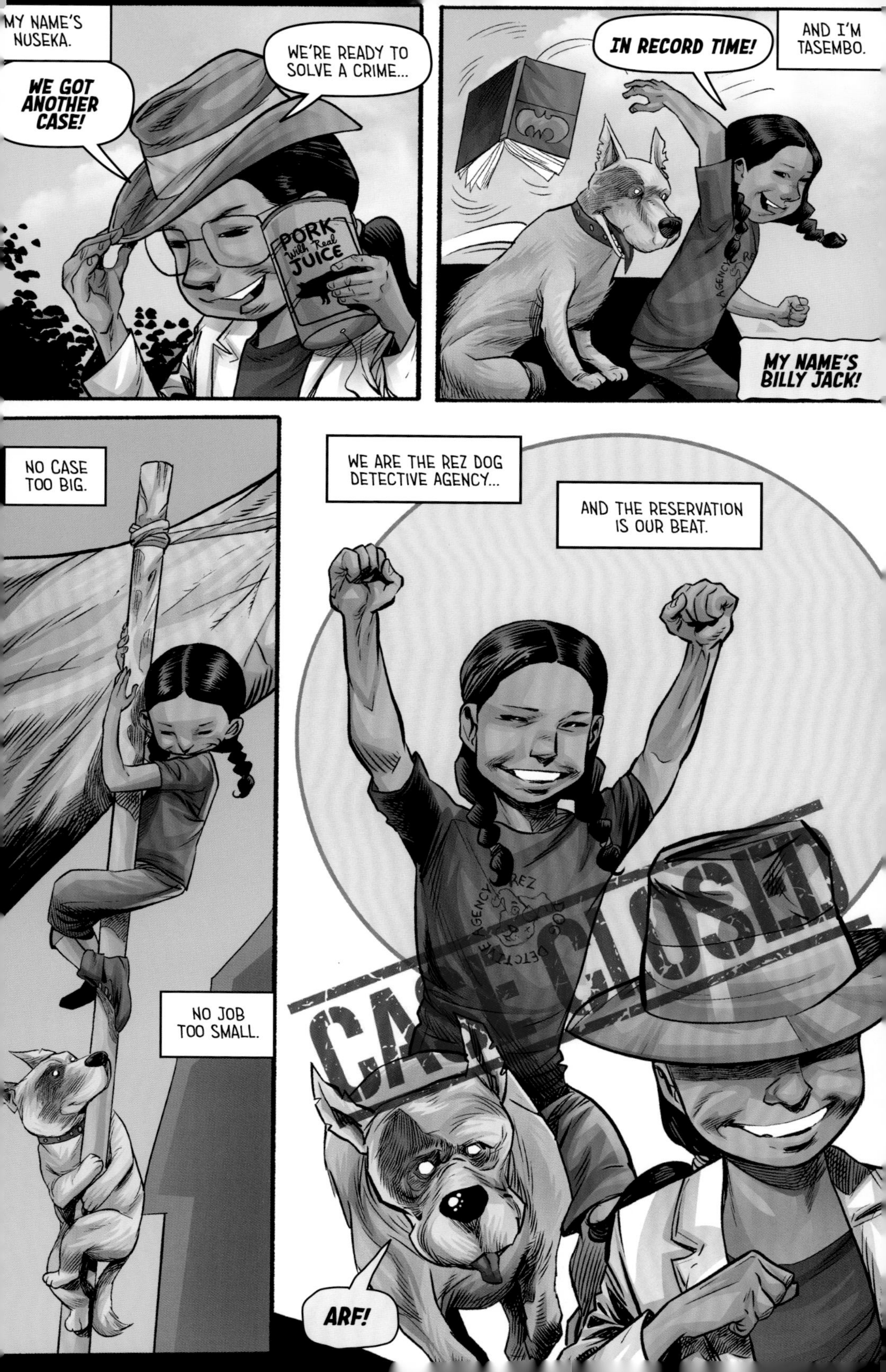

MY NAME'S NUSEKA.
WE GOT ANOTHER CASE!
WE'RE READY TO SOLVE A CRIME...
PORK With Real JUICE
IN RECORD TIME!
AND I'M TASEMBO.
MY NAME'S BILLY JACK!
NO CASE TOO BIG.
NO JOB TOO SMALL.
WE ARE THE REZ DOG DETECTIVE AGENCY...
AND THE RESERVATION IS OUR BEAT.
CASE CLOSED
ARF!

HOW TO MAKE A TIN CUP PHONE

KODEN

(Just like the one the Rez Detectives use at their tree house...er...van.)

What you will need:

1.) Two plastic or paper cups

2.) String. **10-20** feet long.

3.) Tape

4.) Scissors

---> Get help from a guardian when using scissors. <---

A USE THE SCISSORS TO POKE A HOLE IN THE BOTTOM OF THE CUP. RIGHT IN THE CENTER, A HOLE JUST BIG ENOUGH TO PUT THE STRING THROUGH.

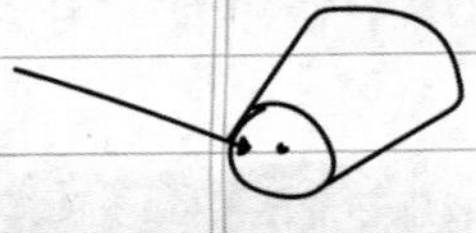

B TIE A KNOT AT THE END OF EACH STRING INSIDE THE CUP. PUT A LITTLE TAPE ON THE STRING TO MAKE SURE IT DOESN'T COME OUT.

TIE KNOT

TAPE

C GIVE ONE OF THE CUPS TO A FRIEND AND WALK AWAY FROM EACH OTHER SLOWLY UNTIL THE STRING IS TIGHT. NOW ONE OF YOU PUT THE CUP TO YOUR EAR AND THE OTHER PERSON TALKS IN THE CUP.

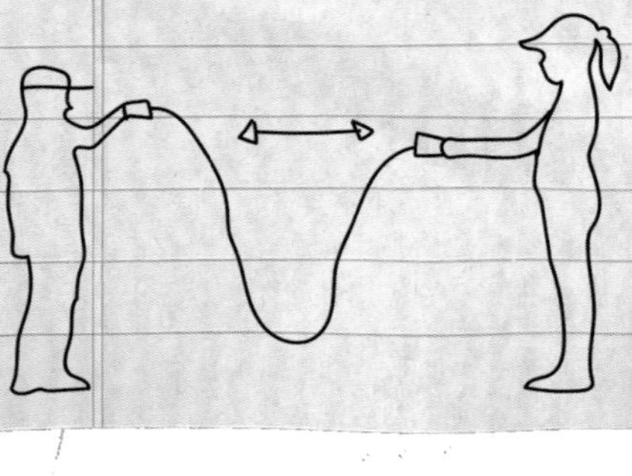

Cool huh!
How does this work?

ALL NOISES ARE ACTUALLY VIBRATIONS. YOUR VOICE MAKES THE AIR PARTICLES START TO VIBRATE, AND THOSE VIBRATION TRAVEL THROUGH THE STRING!

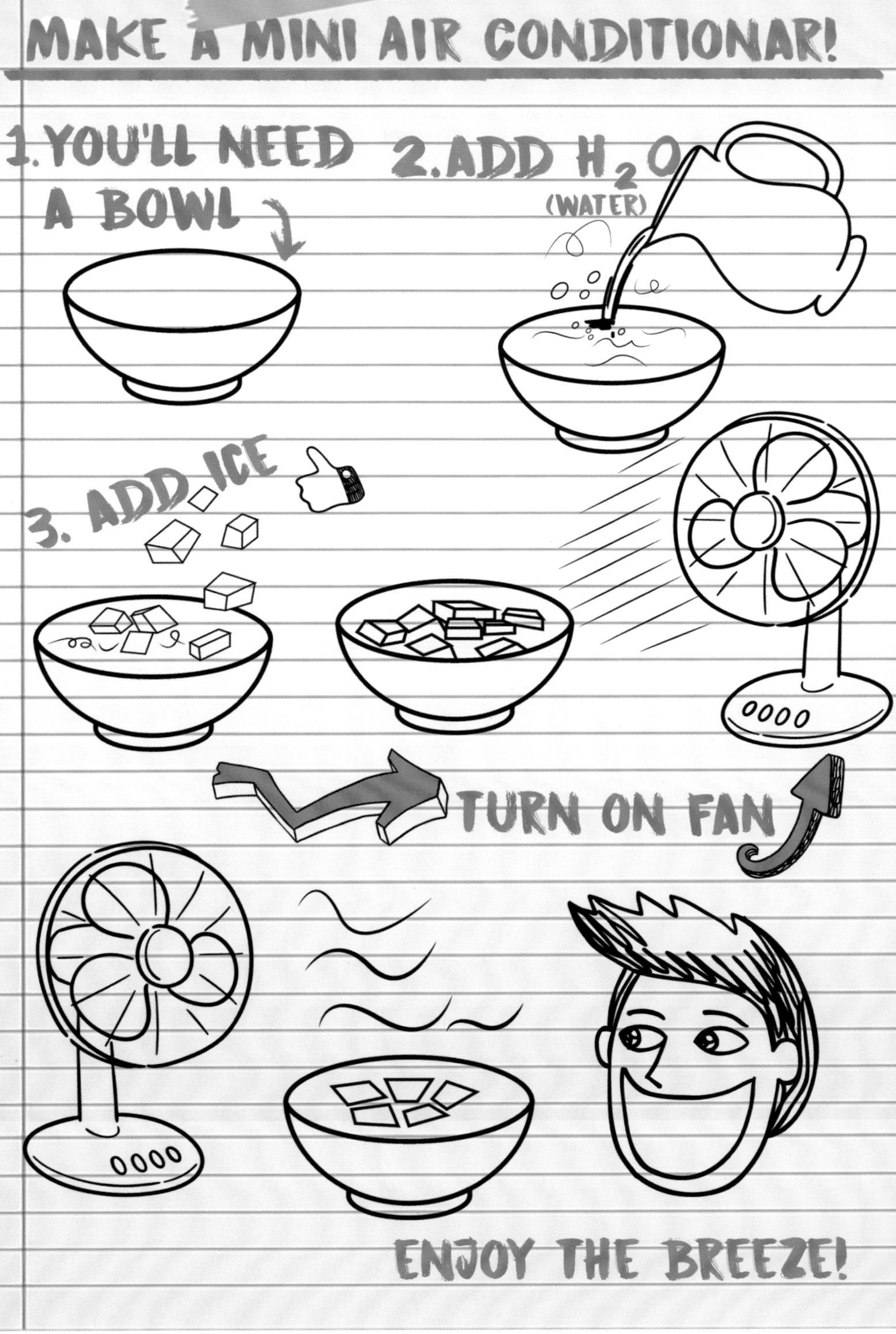
MAKE A MINI AIR CONDITIONAR!
1. YOU'LL NEED A BOWL
2. ADD H_2O
(WATER)
3. ADD ICE
TURN ON FAN
0000
0000
ENJOY THE BREEZE!

Concept Art

V. 1

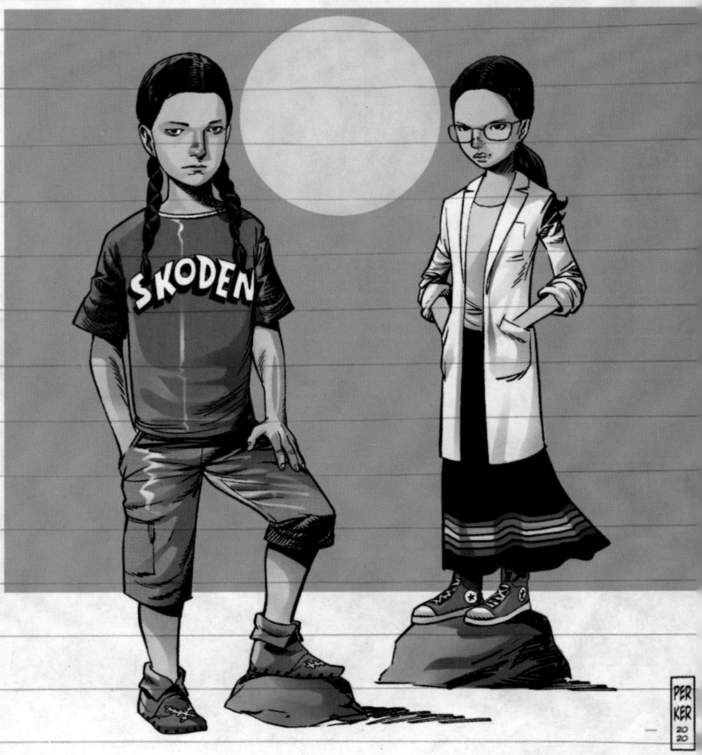
SKODEN
PER KER 20 20

V. 2

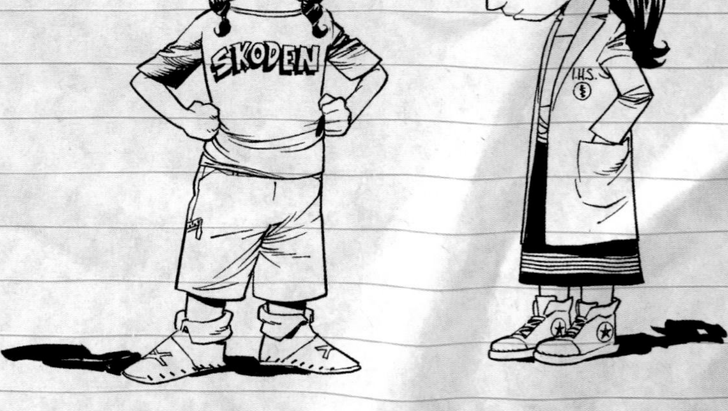
SKODEN
I.H.S.

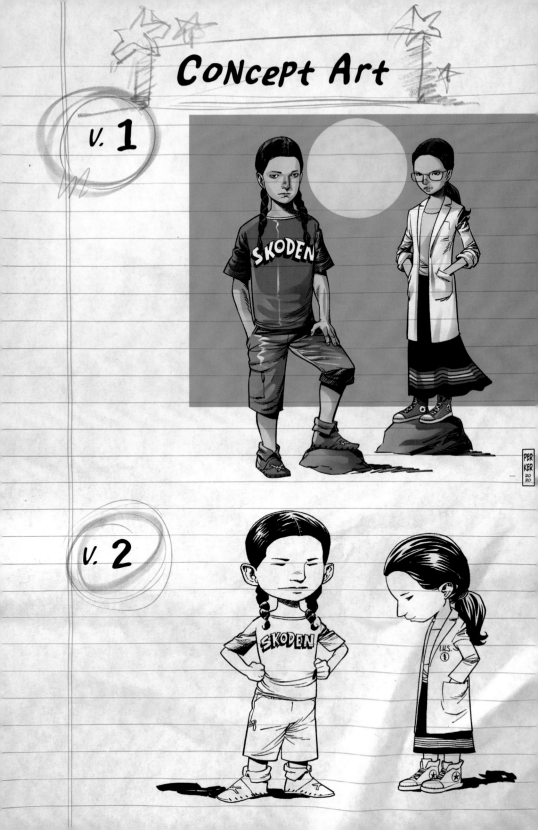

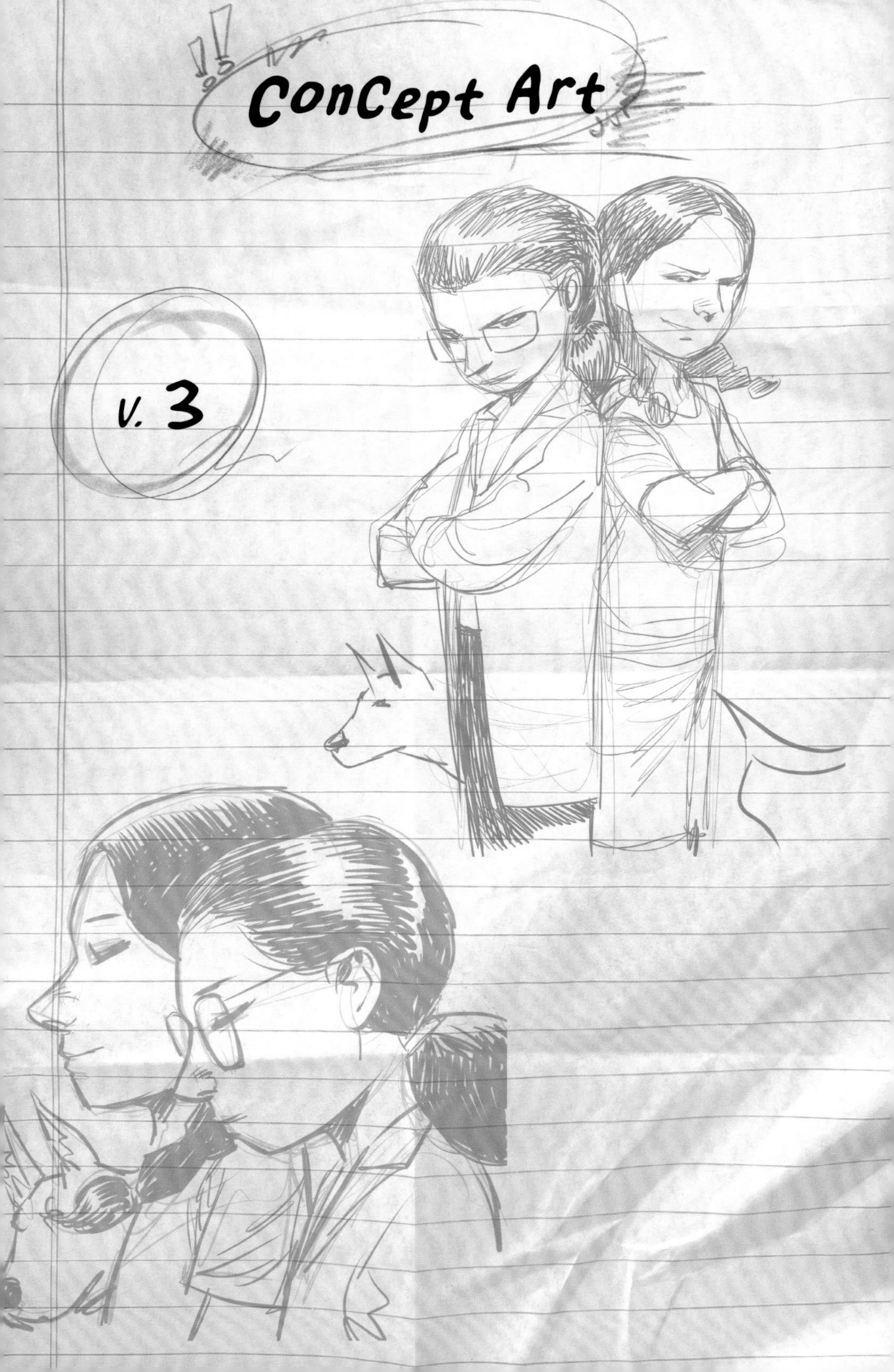
ConCept Art
v. 3

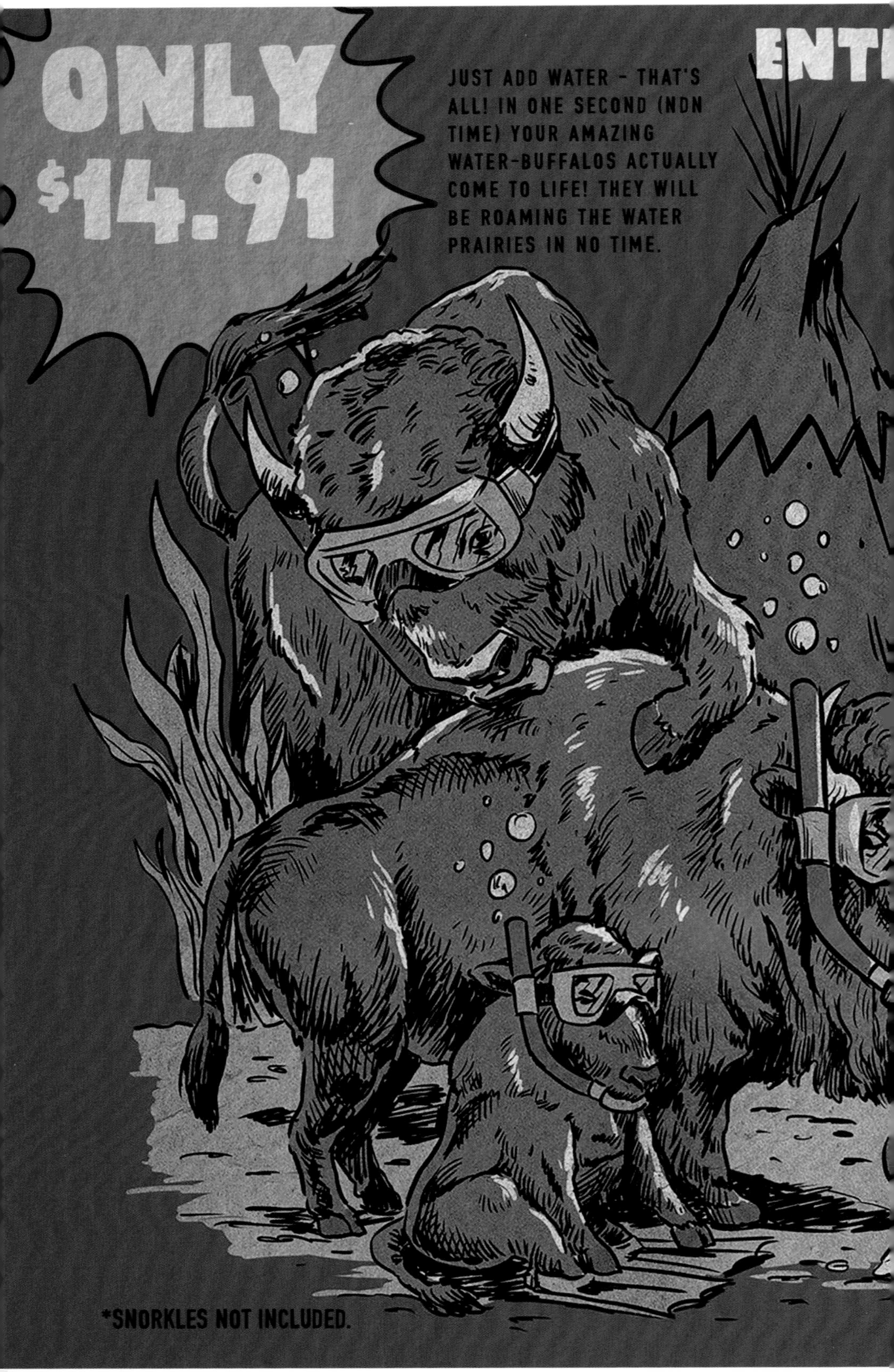
ONLY $14.91
JUST ADD WATER - THAT'S ALL! IN ONE SECOND (NDN TIME) YOUR AMAZING WATER-BUFFALOS ACTUALLY COME TO LIFE! THEY WILL BE ROAMING THE WATER PRAIRIES IN NO TIME.
ENT
*SNORKLES NOT INCLUDED.

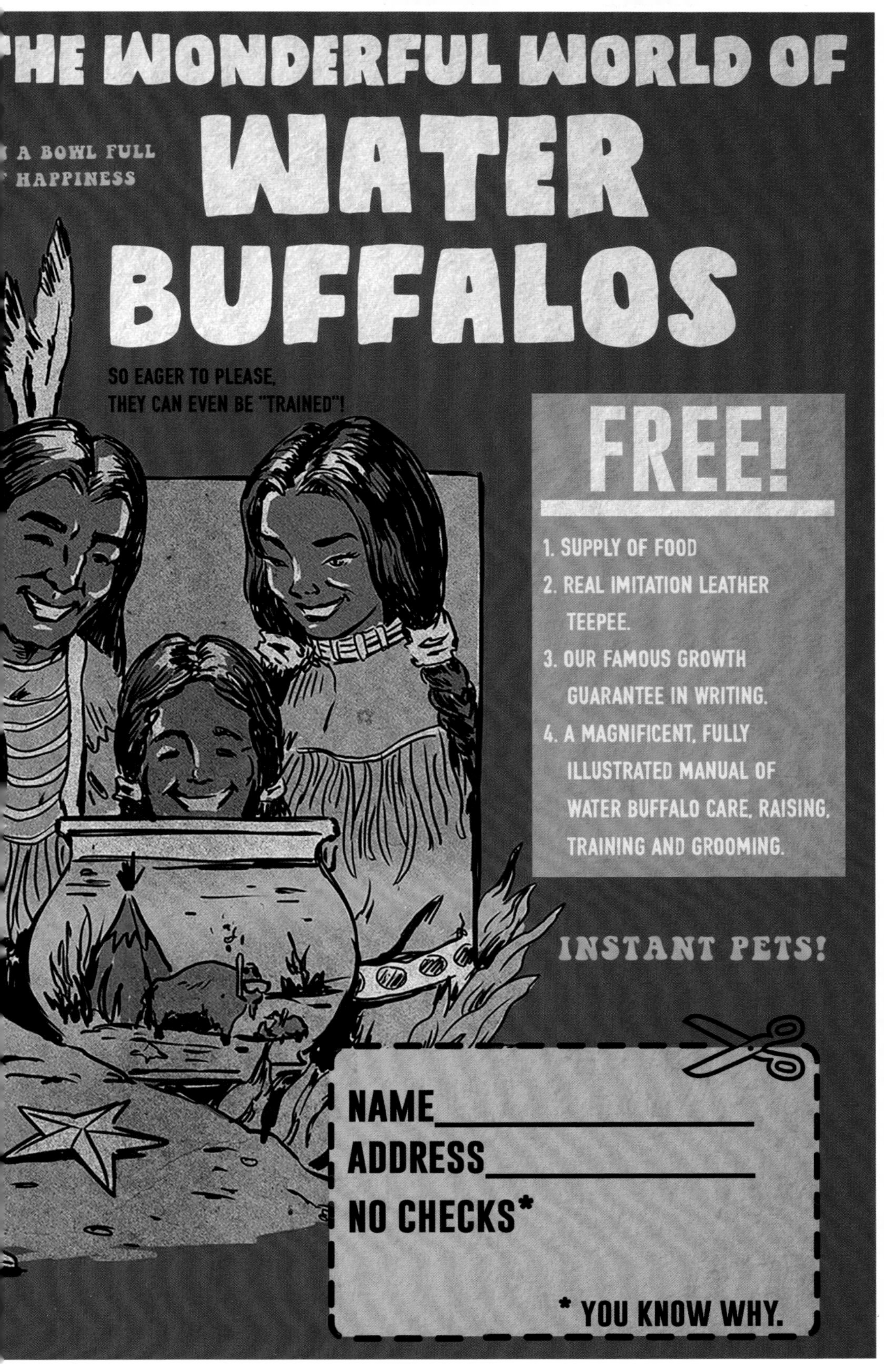

HE WONDERFUL WORLD OF
WATER BUFFALOS
A BOWL FULL
HAPPINESS
SO EAGER TO PLEASE,
THEY CAN EVEN BE "TRAINED"!
FREE!
1. SUPPLY OF FOOD
2. REAL IMITATION LEATHER TEEPEE.
3. OUR FAMOUS GROWTH GUARANTEE IN WRITING.
4. A MAGNIFICENT, FULLY ILLUSTRATED MANUAL OF WATER BUFFALO CARE, RAISING, TRAINING AND GROOMING.
INSTANT PETS!
NAME______________________
ADDRESS__________________
NO CHECKS*
* YOU KNOW WHY.

Acknowledgements

You hear "labor of love" kicked around a lot, but that's truly what this was. We wanted to make a graphic novel that wasn't just "good for a native comic." We wanted it to be objectively good. So we hired an artist in M.K. Perker who has drawn for Marvel, DC, Image, *The New Yorker*, and *MAD* magazine. I want to personally thank you for supporting this book! We're donating this book to some areas that we feel could use it the most. Part of this book was loosely based on a club my brothers and sister and I had when we were kids. We called it "The Rat Cat Gang." So, let's sit back, relax, and go on this little journey with Tasembo, Nuseka, and Billy Jack, the dog.

–Steven Paul Judd

Chi pisa li
Chi haklo li
Chi ikhana li
Chi hullo li

Yakoke goes to...

...The Creator in whatever form you wish to call it for giving us the blessings that we receive, and in alliance with our Creator are we able to tell our stories.

...Literati Press for giving us a place to put this.

...Tulsa library and Broken Bow library for the research material.

...All the talented people who contributed to this book.

...the storytellers, the peace keepers, and all those who inspire.

...The kanomi who are interwoven throughout this book (names and stories and everything else).

...Big ups to our ancestors—those who fought, survived, and inspired us so that we have our rights and our existence, and it is through our stories that we can heal.

–Tvli Jacob

NOW YOU CAN BE A MEMBER OF THE REZ DOG DETECTIVES!

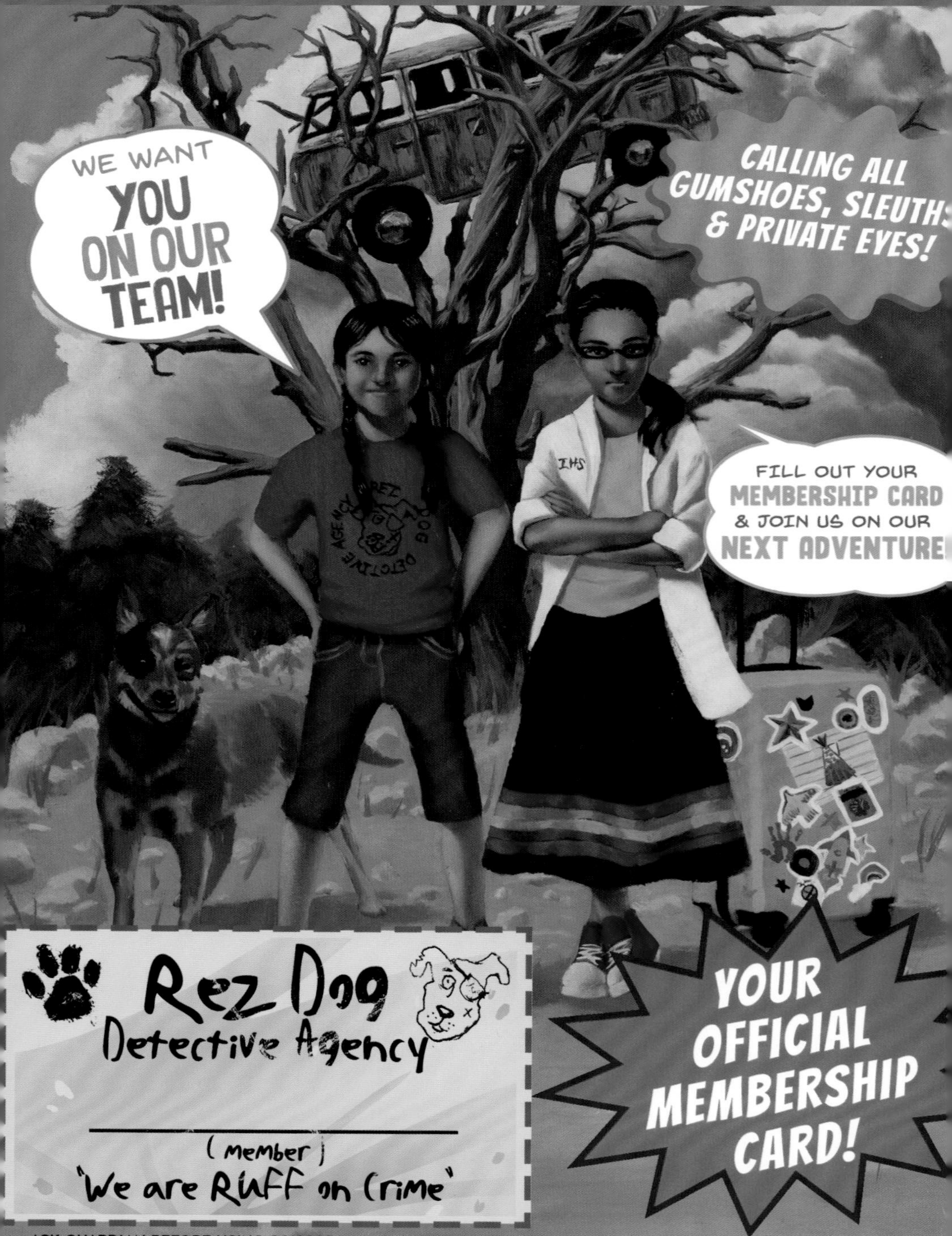
WE WANT YOU ON OUR TEAM!
CALLING ALL GUMSHOES, SLEUTHS & PRIVATE EYES!
FILL OUT YOUR MEMBERSHIP CARD & JOIN US ON OUR NEXT ADVENTURE!
Rez Dog Detective Agency
(member)
"We are RUFF on Crime"
YOUR OFFICIAL MEMBERSHIP CARD!

ASK GUARDIAN BEFORE USING SCISSORS

ART BY CYNTHIA CANADA

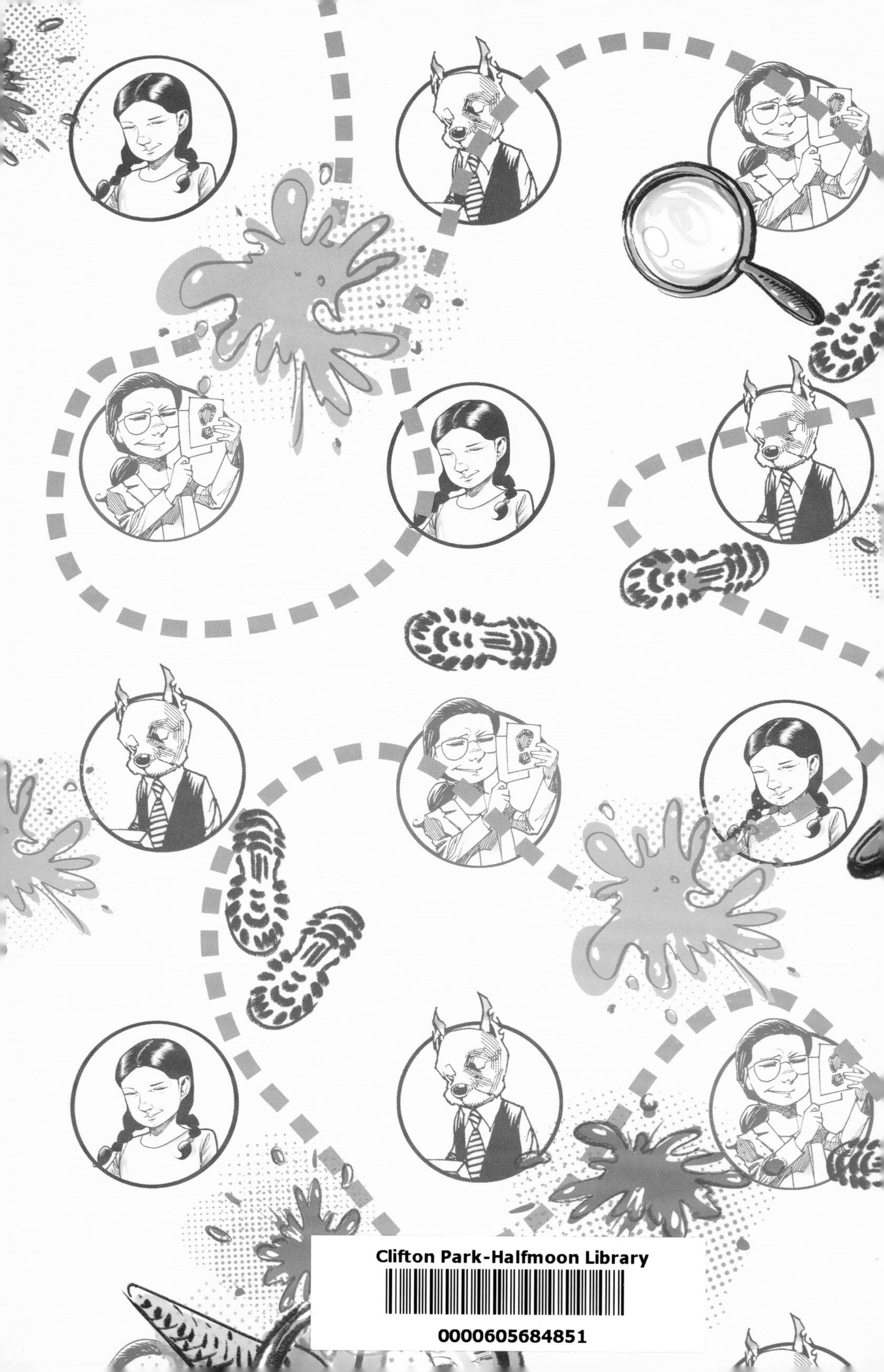